Communicating Like Jesus

A Discovery of the Master's Methods

Terrence W Smith

Edited by Steve Fortosis

ISBN: 1-933899-89-1

Published by:
Holy Fire Publishing
Unit 116
1525-D Old Trolley Rd.
Summerville, SC 29485

www.ChristianPublish.com

Printed in the United States of America and the United Kingdom

Acknowledgements

To my wife Kathy and my children Aaron, Matthew and Rebekah. Thanks for putting up with my many disappearances while writing this book. Thanks to all who helped and all who are mentioned in the book. No one was harmed during its writing. ☺ Thanks especially to my LORD and savior Jesus Christ who is not only the inspiration for great communication, but for eternal and joyous life!

Contents

≈ † ≈

Introduction

After a boring Sunday morning sermon, a friend joked about what the rest of us were thinking, "That message was the best nap I ever had." It seems that such sermons are often associated with things "dry" and "dull". Comments like these reflect one of the most common complaints about Christian communicators, since sermons and lessons no longer create anticipation, nor motivate to participation. "Boring" and "irrelevant" are terms that negatively address a lecture's preparation and presentation. One thing you can be sure of, these complaints were never made by Jesus' or Paul's listeners! Howard Hendricks quipped, "Wherever Paul went they either had a riot or a revival. Wherever I go they serve tea!"[1]

"Jesus and Paul were electrifying without electricity. They incorporated the power of the Spirit, not the power of PowerPoint."

Due to these kinds of sentiments people don't flock into church auditoriums to hear scriptural oratory like they used to or as they should, and according to George Barna's polls, they don't read or study the Scriptures on their own either.[2] The warm pews are found in places of worship that predominately incorporate live drama, lights and spirited contemporary music. But Jesus and Paul were electrifying without electricity. They incorporated the power of the Spirit, not the power of PowerPoint.

So why aren't people engaged by traditional forms of communication? What is the cause of this increasingly rampant boredom? Isn't the Word of God interesting enough to stand on its own, regardless of one's speaking style or expertise?[3] It sure is! For as Isaiah 55:11 states, "So is my word that goes out from my mouth: It will not return to me empty, but will accomplish what I desire and achieve the purpose for which I sent it."

Since God assures the effectiveness of His Word by its own merits, the indifference must be in the preparation and presentation of the message by the presenter. Since the presenter is human (Romans 3:10-14) the product is destined to trouble (Matthew 6:34). Therefore, the message preparation stage needs to exercise prayer, planning and practice in order to be at the place where God would more likely choose to speak through the message and the messenger.

Another problem in our society with all of its mass communication, is miscommunication. In spite of all of the technology we have today, misunderstanding still abounds, possibly more than ever. The following humorous church bulletin misprints are real-life examples of miscommunication:

- Don't let worry kill you, let the church help.

- Thursday night there will be potluck supper. Prayer and medication to follow.

- Remember in prayer the many who are sick of our church and community.

- Tuesday at 4 pm there will be an ice cream social. All ladies giving milk please come early.

- Ladies of the church have cast off clothing of every kind and can be seen in the church basement Friday.

- A bean supper will be held Tuesday evening in the church hall. Music will follow.

- At the evening service tonight, the sermon topic will be "What is hell?" Come early and listen to our choir practice.

One of the reasons I believe mass-communication often breeds miss-communication, is that the average person can only manage so much information. I often tell students that our brains are like sponges. They are designed to soak up information, but they can only soak up a certain amount at a time. With the use of the internet, television, radio, magazines, newspapers, etc., our sponges become dripping wet. So the answer to this memory dilemma, is to soak up less information from the various sources around us and only sponge up (focus on) what is most important.

Where should we go to study effective communication skills and overcome problems like boredom and poor retention? The Bible is the best place to begin. It is replete with great orators and sermons and includes the narratives of the greatest communicator, the Master teacher and preacher, Jesus Christ!

As James S. Stewart aptly penned,

> The teaching of Jesus... has had a power and an effect with which the influence of no other teacher can even be compared. He stands alone - the great Teacher. Readers of the Gospels can but be impressed by the large proportion of His time and strength which Jesus deliberately dedicated to the ministry of teaching. Clearly then it is of the utmost importance that we should study the teaching method of Jesus.[4]

The Gospels[5] record our Lord's self-limited (Philippians 2:6-8) earthly preaching and teaching ministry. In A.T. Robertson's book, "A Harmony of the Gospels" every corresponding verse of each Gospel is offered in side-by-side columns, providing a full account of all the preaching and teaching occurrences by Jesus. An updated version of this harmony is also available in both the NIV and NASB.[6]

In ***Communicating like Jesus***, we will follow His ministry chronologically through the Gospels to discover His expert methodology. It is my prayer that His mode of communication will become ours.

12-13-2006

HE SEEMS TO HAVE LOST HIS ZING

Nic @ Night
Jesus' Encounter with Nicodemus

John 3
1 Now there was a man of the Pharisees named Nicodemus, a member of
the Jewish ruling council. 2 He came to Jesus at night and said, "Rabbi, we
know you are a teacher who has come from God. For no one could
perform the miraculous signs you are doing if God were not with him." 3
In reply Jesus declared, "I tell you the truth, no one can see the kingdom of
God unless he is born again." 4 "How can a man be born when he is old?"
Nicodemus asked. "Surely he cannot enter a second time into his mother's
womb to be born!" 5 Jesus answered, "I tell you the truth, no one can
enter the kingdom of God unless he is born of water and the Spirit. 6
Flesh gives birth to flesh, but the Spirit gives birth to spirit. 7 You should
not be surprised at my saying, `You must be born again.' 8 The wind
blows wherever it pleases. You hear its sound, but you cannot tell where it
comes from or where it is going. So it is with everyone born of the Spirit."
9 "How can this be?" Nicodemus asked. 10 "You are Israel's teacher,"
said Jesus, "and do you not understand these things? 11 I tell you the truth,
we speak of what we know, and we testify to what we have seen, but still
you people do not accept our testimony. 12 I have spoken to you of
earthly things and you do not believe; how then will you believe if I speak
of heavenly things? 13 No one has ever gone into heaven except the one
who came from heaven--the Son of Man. 14 Just as Moses lifted up the
snake in the desert, so the Son of Man must be lifted up, 15 that everyone
who believes in him may have eternal life. 16 "For God so loved the world
that he gave his one and only Son, that whoever believes in him shall not
perish but have eternal life. 17 For God did not send his Son into the
world to condemn the world, but to save the world through him. 18
Whoever believes in him is not condemned, but whoever does not believe
stands condemned already because he has not believed in the name of
God's one and only Son. 19 This is the verdict: Light has come into the
world, but men loved darkness instead of light because their deeds were
evil. 20 Everyone who does evil hates the light, and will not come into the
light for fear that his deeds will be exposed. 21 But whoever lives by the
truth comes into the light, so that it may be seen plainly that what he has
done has been done through God."

He Knew the Scriptures

Nicodemus (Nic) came to Jesus at night either to avoid needless harassment from his colleagues in the Sanhedrin[7], or simply to spend more time with Jesus than he would have been allowed to in the daytime due to the endless crowds of people beginning to follow Christ and encroach on His time. Regardless, the first words Nic uttered to Jesus that night were an acknowledgement of His instructional and spiritual ministry, for he accurately called Him "rabbi" and "teacher" (v. 2). In fact, Jesus is called Rabbi or teacher by other Jewish leaders and individuals as well, and carried out much of His preaching and teaching ministry in the same manner as they did.[8] Furthermore, it is intriguing to realize that this is the first detailed communication encounter[9] of Jesus mentioned in the Gospels and He is preaching[10] to one of Israel's leading teachers and rulers (who later became a believer himself).[11]

Rabbi is a Hebrew term meaning, "master, great one,"[12] and teacher is a Greek word which also means "master" and "teacher."[13] Webster defines a teacher as a person who has knowledge about things and tells them to others.[14] Nic's understanding of Jesus developed because of His reputable knowledge of spiritual things, including a thorough comprehension and retention of the Scriptures. Nic may have even been aware of Jesus' regular attendance at synagogues (Luke 4:16) and the temple (Luke 2:46-47). Traditionally Jewish boys began their formal education in a synagogue school at age six, where they learned to read and write from the Scriptures and do simple math. Then in their secondary years they learned the law, especially the Torah.[15]

A few years ago my family and I took a trip to the Statue of Liberty and Ellis Island. I was fascinated to discover the type of cards that had been produced by the U.S. government to test the English reading comprehension of foreign immigrants—Bible note cards! This was likely due to the Bible's familiarity, respected status and the fact that it had already been translated into more languages than any other piece of literature. The Scriptures were a book of choice, both for the I.N.S. and for Jesus Christ.

If we are to follow Jesus' lifestyle example in this passage, we must acknowledge an immense responsibility to study and know of the Word of God, and to be in places where the Scriptures are carefully taught and preached!

Jesus knew the Scriptures.

He Spent Time in Prayer

In addition to Jesus' ministry of teaching and preaching, Nic also noted where Jesus was from, that He had come "from God" (v. 2). Why did he say this about Jesus? He pointedly stated that it was Christ's signs that brought him to this conclusion, for; "no one could perform the miraculous signs you are doing if God were not with him" (v. 2). The expression "miraculous signs" is actually one Greek word[16] which attests to the miracle worker's authority and that it had been given by God. In this case, it revealed to Nic that Jesus' ministry was God-ordained. These "signs" really pointed to something behind or beyond themselves -- that Jesus really knew God (John 2:11, 23), communed intimately and regularly with His father in Heaven (Luke 5:16), and was God (John 20:30-31).

Jesus was always aware of His mission, and lived every moment in anticipation and preparation. Prayer was His life-line. This kind of lifestyle speaks louder than words ever can! People will gladly listen to the one on whom God's power rests. It seems universally true that the best witness of a believer is his walk, and his works and words will reflect it.

> ***"Anyone who wishes to stand-up with a successful ministry must be willing to bend down in prayer."***

Is there any other way for Christ's disciples to achieve this kind of favor but through continual fervent prayer and the constant study of the Word of God? Note the conditional promise offered in James 4:8, "Draw near to God and He will draw near to you." Oswald Chambers correctly stated, "Prayer does not fit us for greater works, prayer is the greater work."[17] This is why Nic could see clearly that Jesus was a teacher from God. Anyone who wishes to *stand-up* with a successful ministry must be willing to *bend down* in prayer.

Jesus spent time in prayer.

REVERENDFUN.COM COPYRIGHT GG, INC

WHAT ME? ... OH NO, I'M DONE PRAYING ... I THOUGHT YOU WERE STILL PRAYING!

He Met Needs

The miracles themselves would have been a drawing force to Nicodemus' passion to be with Christ. In fact, he stated that none could do them apart from God being with them (v. 2). Since he was a Pharisee and accountable to the Sanhedrin, it would be normal for him to demand a sign[18] for verification of Christ's authenticity. It was an irresistible invitation for him to interact with Jesus. The signs or miracles Jesus performed had likely benefited some of Nic's friends and neighbors in some way, possibly by causing a great deal of rejoicing in many restored families, maybe even his own.

"While turning water into wine… may not be on our "to-do" list, there are many other practical loving ways to help others and share the love of Christ."

Wouldn't most people be anxious to listen to the counsel of this Christ? Wouldn't you? Do we not give more respect and attention to those who have sacrificed greatly for us than to those who have done little or nothing?

Teddy was rough around the edges and didn't care much about schoolwork. He had recently lost his mother and owned a big empty hole in his heart. One Christmas when the children and their teacher were opening gifts to each other, Miss Thompson came to a brown paper bag which was her gift from Teddy. The children laughed at the present, but when she unwrapped it, she acted thankful as she saw a rhinestone bracelet with missing stones and an old bottle of cheap perfume.

Miss Thompson put the bracelet and some perfume on her wrist. She held out her arm and kindly asked the students, "Doesn't it smell lovely?" They got her hint and agreed. After school was over Teddy came up to his teacher's desk and said, "Miss Thompson, you smell just like my mother… and her bracelet looks real pretty on you too. I'm glad you liked my presents." When Teddy left, she got on her knees and asked for God's forgiveness for her failure to see her student's needs before this. This experience changed her perspective on teaching and she now saw her job as a mission field to which she had been called to serve.

Several years later she received a letter from Teddy informing her that he graduated second in his high school class. Four years after that, he wrote again saying that he had graduated first in his college class. Four years later she received the following note;

> Dear Miss Thompson,
>
> As of today I am Theodore Stallard, M.D. How about that? I wanted you to be the first to know I am getting married next month… I want you to come and sit where my mother would sit if she were alive. You are the only family I have now, dad died last year.
>
> Love, Teddy Stallard

When a disciple of Jesus Christ makes this kind of investment and commitment in the life of another, they are respected and honored, maybe even revered! While turning water into wine like Jesus did at the wedding at Cana may not be on your "to-do" list, there are many other practical loving ways to help others and share the love of Christ.

Jesus met needs.

He Hooked Minds with Word Pictures

I remember when I was a boy we used to try to "jig" suckers. These were fresh water bottom feeding fish averaging twelve inches or more and were easily found under the shade of small bridges. They moved slowly and didn't much mind us lowering our hooks down alongside of them to try to jig or hook them on their side. The hooks we used consisted of three hooks welded back to back, so it wasn't that difficult to jig a sucker. The most difficult thing was keeping the fish on the line while pulling it in against its will--it really wasn't interested in cooperating at that point!

Jesus responded to Nic's assessment of Him with a "jig hook" word picture that snagged his curiosity, "No one can see the kingdom of God unless he is *born again*" (v. 3). Nic in turn asked the obvious question about the physical rebirth of a man (vs. 4). Jesus then revealed to him that He was referring to a spiritual birth not a physical one (vv. 5-8). Before Nic realized it, Jesus had sunk his hook in and Nic was contemplating his own spiritual need. Jesus' metaphor[19] spurred an interest in him that had to be pursued.

Jesus' verdict at the end of His encounter with Nic was delivered in the form of an analogy,[20] "Light has come into the world, but men loved darkness instead of light" (v. 19). "Light" obviously represented Jesus and His work of salvation, and "darkness" equaled the opposite -- sin. These were images that Nic could conceptualize and retain for further contemplation.

Later when Jesus instructed on the wisdom of His words, He utilized a simile.[21] He stated, "Therefore everyone who hears these words of mine and puts them into practice is like a wise man who built his house on the rock" (Matthew 7:24).

We would do well to learn to craft such captivating and catching word pictures as Jesus did.

Jesus hooked minds with word pictures.

Thanks to Richard Germain (See Mark 10:25) 01-10-2007

YET ANOTHER ATTEMPT TO FIT A CAMEL THROUGH A NEEDLE

He Answered Relevant Questions

After a crash course on driving the golf cart, my nephew made his own crash course by pushing the accelerator instead of the brake and crashing directly into the back of my VW van. Only Caleb's pride was hurt, but my Vanagon suffered a sixteen-inch long dent. He knew he was supposed to brake before turning on the cart, but he had mistakenly pushed on the wrong pedal.

It certainly wasn't that he hadn't asked enough questions about how to drive before he ventured forward. He was always asking questions. I think he was the most inquisitive ten-year-old I have ever known. The truth is, sometimes when I would see him coming I would think to myself, "Maybe I'd better stay out of sight, I have too much to think about right now to answer a thousand questions."

As Caleb got older, his questions became more sensible and practical. The funny thing is, his persistent curiosity has led to many successes he has experienced as a young adult. By the age of twenty-two, with the completion of a college degree and pilot's license, he began managing a municipal airport.

Nicodemus asked a relevant question of Jesus by inquiring how a person could be born again (vs. 9). Note the fact that Jesus directly gave him a direct reply (vs. 10). He certainly did not have to or need to, but He did. He, the Creator (Colossians 1:15-17) of the universe, the King of kings and Lord of lords (1 Timothy 6:14b-15; Revelation 17:14; 19:15) took the time to answer this man's questions and used it as a teachable moment.[22]

How much more should we be aware of the questions people are asking and be ready to give solid Biblical answers (1 Peter 3:15)!

There were times when Jesus answered questions with a question and occasions when He didn't answer the question at all! These two options can be seen in Matthew 21:23-27 when Jesus is asked about His authority by the teachers of the law. He replied by asking them a question about John the Baptist's ministry that they couldn't answer directly for fear of admission of His authority (v. 5) and fear of the people (v. 6). So they simply retorted they didn't know the answer. Consequently, Jesus withheld His answer by stating, "Neither will I tell you by what authority I am doing these things" (v. 8).

The questions Jesus appreciated and answered were those that supported His assignment. He never got caught up in foolish and senseless arguments. The apostle Paul rein-forced Jesus' position when he wrote to Timothy, his son in the faith, "Don't have anything to do with foolish and stupid arguments, because you know they produce quarrels. 24 And the Lord's servant must not quarrel; instead, he must be kind to everyone, able to teach…" (2 Timothy 5:23).

Jesus answered relevant questions.

IF GOD REALLY LOVES US WHY WOULD HE ALLOW SIN ... AND WHILE WE'RE ON THE SUBJECT, SLOW MODEMS?

He Appealed to Truth

I purposefully burned my friend's arm. Now I know it sounds too incredible to believe or maybe after thinking about it you will conclude I am one of Stephen King's inspirations or cohorts. After all, we do only live a couple miles from each other. No, let me assure you it's not that bad. Before I explain my sadistic behavior, let me back up a little ways.

In the early 70's, Christians were not afraid to talk about Hell and its reality for lost souls. It seemed like most everyone believed in it anyway and were consequently given to reasonable moral living. The certainty of hell was the theme of many a Gospel message and the funny thing is, I don't recall the last time I've heard one!

Hearing of the Lake of Fire at a CEF (Child Evangelism Fellowship) backyard Bible study was the subject that caught my attention as an unsaved 11- or 12-year-old boy and resulted in my coming to Christ. I was so convinced by the power of its truth that I was eager to tell my friends.

While at church camp with an unsaved friend that summer, we heard a hellfire and brimstone message and I asked him what he thought about becoming a Christian. He replied that he didn't care if he went to hell or not. That response shocked me so much it just wouldn't do--so I experimented with one of my "How to Lose Friends and Make Enemies" tactics. I snuck up behind him when he wasn't looking and lit a lighter under his arm. It was very effective—but only at getting his attention and making him very angry with me! I asked him if he enjoyed that sensation, because if he didn't ask Jesus to save him, he could look forward to a whole lot more of it in the future.

I was appealing to truth with my friend with the right motives, but definitely the wrong methods. At that time I did know about "speaking the truth in love" (Ephesians 4:15). Fortunately, when Jesus appealed to truth, He did it differently.

When answering Nic's questions, Jesus petitioned for truth three times. Note verses 3, 5, and 11 where Jesus stated, "I tell you the truth..." Being God and already recognized as a Rabbi, He did not need to lobby for truth or anything else for that matter, yet He did so just the same. He obviously wanted Nic to understand His message. In the case of human speakers, truth is a higher authority than themselves and very effective in winning a group's respect and attention. A much-sought-after-prize by great thinkers and philosophers throughout history.

Jesus is recorded using this phrase, "I tell you the truth," 30 times in Matthew's Gospel, 14 times in Mark's Gospel, 9 times in Luke's Gospel, and 29 times in John's Gospel. The Word "truth" is used by itself an additional 17 times in the Gospel of John alone.

Jesus often used physical truths to explain spiritual ones. When He used the word picture "born-again" with Nicodemus, He wanted Nic's understanding of human birth to be a bridge so Nic could cross over to a comprehension of spiritual birth and its necessity in entering heaven.

In verse 13 Jesus stated that, "No one has ever gone into heaven." Nic was not going to dispute this truth unless of course he thought of Enoch (Genesis 5:24; Hebrews 11:5) or Elijah (2 Kings 2:13). However, Nic knew that these men were caught up to heaven by God, and Jesus was claiming that He would *take Himself* to heaven, "except the one who came from heaven--the Son of Man" (v. 13b). So Jesus used a physical reality to help Nic understand a spiritual truth.

Obviously truth was significantly important to Jesus as a foundation for His teaching ministry. It would seem apparent then, that any serious Christian communicator should focus on and share truth as a base for their communications also.

Jesus appealed to truth.

REVERENDFUN.COM COPYRIGHT GCI, INC

Thanks to Alonzo Myers 07-27-2006

YOU, MOST OF ALL, CAN'T HANDLE THE TRUTH

He Repeated and Reviewed

Marketing experts tell us that when we want to advertise an event that gets attention, we should make contact with our prospective clients about seven times.[23] They say that if we are using direct marketing mailings, the average person just begins to notice our materials by about the third or fourth piece of correspondence. The recipient is likely to put all email and snail-mail in file thirteen (the trash) until they become familiar with the sender. The advertising world knows the value of repetition and review in order to build interest in a product. Christian ministries can learn a lot from them.

I have thought often about my ability to recall messages, lessons or lectures, and besides those that were creative and memorable, the ones that I have been able to remember the best, have involved repetition and review. Sometimes the studies were offered as acrostics like "ACTS" for the components of prayer (adoration, confession, thanksgiving and supplication), or occasionally, simple three point sermons using alliteration like, "His Purpose, Plan and Power for Ministry." When the preacher or teacher reviewed often during their oratory, it would cause better retention in the listener.

Jesus used similar tactics as He repeated, reviewed and rephrased His thoughts regularly in His speaking. In verse 3 He proclaimed that Nic needed to be "*born* again," in order to see the Kingdom of Heaven. Then, He repeated the phrase again in verse 7. In verses 5 and 8 He stated that Nic must be "*born* of the Spirit." Four times Jesus discussed this new concept of a spiritual birth with

Nicodemus. Jesus then sermonized for the next eleven verses about the heart of the Gospel. The reason I consider this a sermon rather than a lesson or a counseling session, is that the Gospel is the focus of this message, not doctrine or Christian growth.

A carefully detailed study of all the places where the word "preach" and its various forms are used in the New Testament revealed that it meant, "to proclaim, herald and publish" a particular message, and is used almost entirely in relationship with the Gospel.[24] Thus the message of preaching in the New Testament is the Gospel message. On the other hand, the words for "teach" in the New Testament have to do with "instruction, doctrine and explanation," and deal primarily with Christian growth, or discipleship.[25]

Jesus often repeated or rephrased his points. It would make sense for us to do the same so that listeners will retain what they have heard.

Jesus repeated and reviewed.

He Provoked Thinking

Most of us don't care for confrontation of any kind but we sure do sit up and pay close attention when someone else is fighting or being confronted. In fact, I have heard folks say things like, "I sure enjoy a good fight." Sometimes my most memorable Sunday school classes were those that turned into verbal and emotional battles between two opposing doctrinal foes. Was a sense of community and camaraderie enhanced by it? No, but we sure paid attention to the teaching method (although likely unplanned)!

In verse 7 it appears Jesus planned His wrangle. He must have provoked Nic's emotions and intellect for He said, "You should not be surprised at my saying, 'You must be born again.'" Jesus knew that Nic was well learned and even referred to him as "Israel's teacher" in verse 10. The statement, "You should not be surprised," suggests that Nic should have been aware of the concept of spiritual birth and Jesus was simply attempting to stimulate Nic's mind through verbal incitement. It may not always be appropriate to use this method for communicating truth, but it certainly was effective with this teacher of Israel.

Jesus also used strange facts to entice deeper thinking among His audience. Just before Jesus sends the disciples out to do ministry in pairs in Matthew chapter 10, He instructs them on God's protection and provision. He tells them that God has them in His care and that, "even the very hairs" of their heads "are numbered" (v. 30). This must have seemed an odd fact to the disciples, but it certainly would have caused them to further peruse the concept of God's love for them.

Jesus also introduced startling and unsettling concepts. When He taught His disciples about causing others to stumble in Matthew 18, He proclaimed, "if your hand or your foot causes you to sin cut it off and throw it away… if your eye causes you to sin, gouge it out and throw it away" (v. 9). Clearly He was not instructing them to maim themselves, but to realize the need for self-discipline, control, and making sure that others would not miss the Kingdom of Heaven because of them. This statement surely grabbed their attention like few others would!

In Luke 12 Jesus informed the disciples and the crowds that were present that they should look for His return. He said they should be ready in the same way that servants of that day were always to be ready for their master's return from a wedding banquet to unlock and open his door for him. Jesus said it would be a good experience for those who were ready, but announced an alarming consequence for the unprepared servant in His illustration: "He will cut him to pieces and assign him a place with the unbelievers." For those who simply did not do their master's will, a beating of many blows was planned. The simple understanding of this parable is that severe punishment awaits the disobedient servants.

It is hard to imagine what must have been coursing through the minds of the group. What was this Rabbi of love and healing talking about? How could He be so crass and cruel? Whatever the case, He had successfully stirred their consciousness and secured their attention!

Upon nearing the end of His earthly ministry, Jesus

spent more time in confrontation with the Pharisees and the teachers of the law. He announced seven woes to them in Matthew 23, confronting their teaching, challenging their actions, and calling them names! Jesus used ten derogatory names in this passage, calling them: "hypocrites" six times (vv. 13, 15, 23, 25, 27, 29); "son of hell" (v. 15); "blind fools" (v. 17); "blind men" (v. 19); "blind guides" (v. 24); "blind Pharisee" (v. 26); "white-washed tombs" (v. 27); "snakes" (v. 33); and "brood of vipers" (v. 33).

Obviously there would be few occasions today when Christ's disciples would need to joust with such pointed verbal swords, yet it remains significant that the Master communicator found occasion to wield so. This extreme tactic definitely pierces the flesh of a self-righteous and self-glorifying existence.

Jesus provoked thinking.

He Used Familiar Illustrations

Billy Graham used to say that it was only reasonable to believe in a God we can't see; after all, there are lots of things we can't see or have never seen that exist just the same. He suggested we take the wind as an example. You can't see it, but you can see its affects, just as you can't see God, but you can see His work and His Spirit's work in changed lives. Some were murderers, thieves, liars, drunks, and more, and they metamorphosed into something new and pure because of the regenerating work of the Holy Spirit.

Probably Dr. Graham borrowed this familiar illustration from Jesus Himself who explained to Nicodemus the work of the Spirit in verse 8. Everyone knows about the wind: its unpredictably sporadic changes of direction and how it is heard and not seen. It is evidence of something truly existing even though humans cannot visually observe it. God, the Holy Spirit can be seen by His effects on us (2 Corinthians 5:17) and the created order (Romans 1:20). This very simple illustration caused Nic to further investigate the matter by asking another question about the Spirit of God (v. 9).

Jesus referred to common natural world occurrences on a number of occasions. In Luke 12:54-56 He said to the listening crowd, "When you see a cloud rising in the west, immediately you say, 'It's going to rain,' and it does, and when the south wind blows, you say, 'It's going to be hot,' and it is." This illustration of the weather was something they discussed daily. Jesus, thus, built a bridge in their minds enabling them to perceive the truth about their lack of understanding of "the times."

People generally want to be able to understand spiritual things. In his polling of Americans, George Barna discovered that today's un-churched "...are seeking an understanding of the religious core of the church"[26] and "Befriending God... is important to most Americans, even for those who do not see the value of church life."[27] This attitude agrees with Paul's teaching to the Corinthians that everyone has a conscience (2 Corinthians 4:2) and to the Romans that God has revealed Himself to every one (Romans 1:19-20).

"Familiar examples are incredibly effective at making uncommon things comprehensible."

One of the biggest barriers preventing seekers from finding what they are looking for is our poor communication of what our churches are about, who we are in Christ and how the Bible describes God. Since people want to befriend God and understand the Church, we ought to actively be seeking familiar ways to connect with them and relate the true message of peace with God.

Familiar examples are incredibly effective at making uncommon things comprehensible. Let's put them to use like Jesus did and help others to connect with Him through us.

Jesus used familiar illustrations.

(See 1Thessalonians 5:1-3) 11-25-1999

LIKE A THIEF IN THE NIGHT YOU NEVER KNOW WHEN YOUR TIME ON THIS EARTH WILL RUN OUT

He Built Others Up

The sound it made was so strange. I had never heard anything like it before. It sounded like a cross between a loud quick release of air and a sledge hammer hitting a dumpster from a distance.

It was about 4:30 in the morning and I had to get up and discover what was making that intermittent clanging. If I had one hundred guesses, I never would have picked this one. As I walked up to the kitchen window I was shocked to see the infirmary of the church camp for which I was the director, burned to the ground! Or should I say "not see" it since it was no longer there! The only thing left was a propane tank sporadically spewing flames in the direction of the former structure. All that remained were burning embers from the floor joists and the flame-throwing tank.

Since the tank's pressure relief valve was working properly, the tank did not blow up in the night as the Fire Marshal suggested could have happened. Somehow the valve's exhaust port got pointed toward the building, and that is what encouraged the rapid burning of the infirmary.

Jesus further fanned the flame of Nic's thinking by addressing his sense of self-worth through acknowledgement and affirmation of his position and accomplishments. This can be seen in verse 10 where Jesus comments that Nic was "Israel's teacher."

People love to be encouraged and affirmed. For Christians, encouragement is a command. 1 Thessalonians 5:10 reads, "Therefore encourage one another and build each other up, just as in fact you are doing." In Hebrews 3:13 we find that encouragement is an important factor in aiding others to live a holy life, "But encourage one another daily, as long as it is called today, so that none of you may be hardened by sin's deceitfulness." The results of a lack of encouragement can be disastrous.

Some preachers tear apart individuals or groups in their sermons because of disagreements over theology or ministry practice. Jesus however, employed affirmation and encouragement in His approach (with the exception of the hypocritical religious leaders as mentioned earlier). Should we His servants do any less?

In John 13 Jesus was preparing the disciples for His suffering and death and opened His heart to them. He told them to love as He had loved them and called them His children. For most parents, their children are their most precious and dearest treasure. Their love for them is like God's sacrificial love for us. They, too, (for the most part) would give their lives for their children. Jesus loved the world enough to give His life and to call the disciples His children! This was a term of endearment and affection, and certainly must have boosted their trust and love for their Master!

Jesus built others up.

He Asked Questions

Along with the affirmation Jesus gave Nicodemus, came a very pointed question, "Do you not understand these things" (v. 10)? This was a sharp inquiry based on Nic's position as a teacher, and had the potential of cutting and offending. Yet since it was coupled with the affirmation of his position, it was apparently accepted by Nic without any problems.[28] In fact, we later read that Nic stood up for Jesus at a meeting of the Sanhedrin (John 7:50) and accompanied Joseph of Arimathea at Christ's burial (John 19:39). There are times when direct and pointed questions are helpful in driving a point home.

Take notice as well that this question in verse 10, was in reply to a question. Jesus often responded to questions with another question to cause further and deeper thinking of the really important issue(s). In Mark's Gospel Jesus responded to the inquiry of paying taxes with three questions (Mark 12:13-17). Their reply to His questions answered their own. When Jesus asked Nic about his lack of understanding, the question certainly must have stimulated his thought processes. Good communicators craft questions that help their listeners discover many of the answers on their own!

It is amazing how much Jesus used inquiry with the highly educated and wealthy Nicodemus. In verse 12 He used a rhetorical question, which is defined as "one put for effect and not requiring an answer."[29] He said, "I have spoken to you of earthly things and you do not believe; how then will you believe if I speak of heavenly things?"

Rhetorical questions served Jesus' purposes in delivering spiritual truth.

According to Clifford Wilson, Jesus used questions for at least twelve different purposes.[30] In addition to those already discussed, Jesus used questions to *clarify people's thinking* on particular matters, such as in Mark 10:3 where He asked, "What did Moses command you?" reminding them of their responsibility to the Torah.

Some questions *expressed an emotion* like His response to the Pharisees in Matthew 12:34, "How can you, being evil, speak what is good?"

Jesus *introduced illustrations with inquiry*, "Suppose one of you has a friend..." (Luke 11:5-6). He even utilized this type of question with Nicodemus in verses 12-14 where He talks about Moses lifting up the snake in the wilderness as it related to Himself soon to be lifted up on the cross.

Wilson writes that some questions were *used for emphasizing a point*, as in Matthew 16:24, "What good will it be for a man if he gains the whole world, yet forfeits his soul? Or what can a man give in exchange for his soul?" Other questions can *aid in the application of truth*, like the question Jesus asked after telling the parable of the good Samaritan; "Which of these three do you think was a neighbor to the man who fell into the hands of robbers" (Luke 10:36)?

Inquiries were occasionally made simply *to retrieve information.* This was the case in Matthew 15:34 when Jesus asked the boy how many loaves he had.

Relationships were established by the use of questions; Jesus asked the crowd when the woman drew healing power from Him, "Who touched me" (Luke 8:35)?

Some questions were asked *to silence or rebuke His opponents*;

> "John's baptism--where did it come from? Was it from heaven, or from men?" They discussed it among themselves and said, "If we say, `From heaven,' he will ask, `Then why didn't you believe him?' 26 But if we say, `From men'--we are afraid of the people, for they all hold that John was a prophet." 27 So they answered Jesus, "We don't know." Then he said, "Neither will I tell you by what authority I am doing these things (Matthew 21:25-27).

Jesus also formed questions *that brought conviction* as He did in Mark 2:25: "Have you never read what David did when he and his companions were hungry and in need?"

Finally, some of His questions were *examinations*; Jesus asked, "Simon, son of John, do you love me" (John 21:15-17)?

Questions demand answers. The right questions should initiate serious thinking by the hearer. That alone is a major accomplishment these days.

Jesus asked questions.

He Used the Scriptures

You have seen them--maybe there is one in your family or neighborhood. We call them savers or packrats. Some prefer to call themselves collectors. They save everything and anything. From plastic bags (hundreds of them) and old yellowed newspapers to clothes that haven't been worn in over 30 years. My dad even saves the lids off of frozen juice cans for use as coasters under furniture legs. Why he needs five thousand of them for one couch and one chair is beyond me!

I think most of us could tell humorous stories about such individuals with varying opinions as to the value of their or even our own "stuff." The truth is, some homes are outright fire hazards, while others have too little space left to even entertain a friendly visitor. But is this stuff any good if it is never used?

Earlier I stated that Jesus knew the Scriptures. We will now observe that He didn't let that knowledge just sit around in His head and collect dust--He utilized it. Paul under the inspiration of the Holy Spirit affirmed their holy use when he wrote to Timothy his son in the faith and urged him to do his best to study and "correctly handle the Word of truth" (2 Timothy 2:15).

In the very next chapter he added that the Bible is breathed out by God and "useful for teaching, rebuking, correcting and training in righteousness, 17 so that the man of God may be thoroughly equipped for every good work" (2 Timothy 3:16-17). There is no question that the Bible is meant to be known and used by all God's children and the result is righteous living (John 14:15) and good work that brings glory to God (Ephesians 2:10).

Paul gave great authority and responsibility to young Timothy because of his knowledge and faithful use of the Scriptures. This was a rare occurrence in the Jewish community of the first century, as elders were usually "elder" men. It began a trend in the Church to use men as elders who were "elders" in the faith and familiar with the Word of God and the Holy Spirit's work and guidance in the Church.

In verse 14 Jesus offered a prophecy of His death on the cross (not a challenge to praise Him as many think this passage suggests); just as Moses had lifted up the snake in the desert so He needed to be "lifted up." His methodology of choice here was Biblical reference. Jesus referred to an account only recorded in the Scriptures, and as mentioned earlier, this kind of teaching is reinforced by God directly (Isaiah 55:11).

God blesses the reading of His Word[31] and those who desire God to work through them must use His Word often in their preparation, preaching and practice. The first point learned from Jesus' encounter with Nicodemus was the need to know the Word; here the need to utilize it contextually is clearly evidenced.

Jesus used the Scriptures.

EVERYONE PLEASE BROWSE TO BIBLE.GOSPELCOM.NET AND BRING UP PSALMS FOR TODAY'S SCRIPTURE READING

He Got to the Point

Most Americans are increasingly skeptical of political speeches and lengthy legal jargon that seems written only for lawyers and politicians. After all the scandals in government in recent years, a fresh, honest, and right-to-the-point voice would be welcomed and appreciated.

After Jesus had spoken briefly with Nicodemus, He gave him the heart of His message; "that everyone who believes in Him may have eternal life" (v. 15). Communicators who are disciples of Jesus Christ should share in His simple directness.

Another time, when Jesus was teaching in the temple courts (in John 8), He made further direct statements which almost got Him killed. The Jewish people claimed Abraham as their father and then God as their father, and Jesus responded, "If God were your Father, you would love me, for I came from God and now am here. I have not come on my own; but he sent me" (v. 42). Later, in verse 55, He exclaimed, "Your father Abraham rejoiced at the thought of seeing my day," and "before Abraham was born, I am" (v. 58)! That was about as direct as He could get. Jesus spared no punches in explaining His purpose and identity to them. His explanation was so clear they considered it blasphemy and "picked up stones to stone Him" (v. 58).

Many preachers are capable of stirring up a torrent of words with gale-force emotion, but leave no debris of nourishment for soaking into the fertile ground of the human mind and soul! If the main point of a message really is the most important element, then it must be prioritized and delivered efficiently and effectively.

Jesus got to the point.

Thanks to Joy Garman 03-26-2007

ONCE PASTOR DAVE NAILED THE PERFECT SERMON, THE SPONSORSHIPS FINALLY STARTED ROLLING IN

He Summarized

I remember when I first discovered "Coles Notes" in high school; for me it was the end of my struggle to understand Shakespeare. What an educational breakthrough! I was finally able to grasp the meaning of that antiquated English and write critically and credibly as my teacher demanded. It actually became fun for me! All I needed was a few summary points and statements which proved to clarify William's poetic ideas.

As a conclusion to His meeting with Nicodemus, Jesus summarized and simplified His thesis, offering Nic His Rabbinic "verdict,"-- people love "darkness", but the "light" has come to set them free (v. 19). Since Jesus spoke of "heavenly things" Nicodemus had difficulty understanding, so Jesus provided a simple and plain summary for him. The result was that Jesus' spoken message was clear and simple, just as He said spiritual truth should be "seen plainly" (v. 21).

"Whether or not Jesus needed to plan His messages, one thing is certain, He used a variety of means with which to deliver them."

More than a dozen principles of communication were implemented by Jesus in His encounter with Nicodemus. Whether or not Jesus needed to plan His messages, one thing is certain, He used a variety of means with which to deliver them. Obviously He wanted them to be received and understood.

Jesus summarized.

Getting Well At the Well

Jesus' Encounter with the Woman at the Well

<u>John 4</u>

5 So he came to a town in Samaria called Sychar, near the plot of ground
Jacob had given to his son Joseph. 6 Jacob's well was there, and Jesus,
tired as he was from the journey, sat down by the well. It was about the
sixth hour. 7 When a Samaritan woman came to draw water, Jesus said to
her, "Will you give me a drink?" 8 (His disciples had gone into the town to
buy food.) 9 The Samaritan woman said to him, "You are a Jew and I am a
Samaritan woman. How can you ask me for a drink?" (For Jews do not
associate with Samaritans.) 10 Jesus answered her, "If you knew the gift of
God and who it is that asks you for a drink, you would have asked him and
he would have given you living water." 11 "Sir," the woman said, "you
have nothing to draw with and the well is deep. Where can you get this
living water? 12 Are you greater than our father Jacob, who gave us the
well and drank from it himself, as did also his sons and his flocks and
herds?" 13 Jesus answered, "Everyone who drinks this water will be thirsty
again, 14 but whoever drinks the water I give him will never thirst. Indeed,
the water I give him will become in him a spring of water welling up to
eternal life." 15 The woman said to him, "Sir, give me this water so that I
won't get thirsty and have to keep coming here to draw water." 16 He told
her, "Go, call your husband and come back." 17 "I have no husband," she
replied. Jesus said to her, "You are right when you say you have no
husband. 18 The fact is, you have had five husbands, and the man you
now have is not your husband. What you have just said is quite true." 19
"Sir," the woman said, "I can see that you are a prophet. 20 Our fathers
worshiped on this mountain, but you Jews claim that the place where we
must worship is in Jerusalem." 21 Jesus declared, "Believe me, woman, a
time is coming when you will worship the Father neither on this mountain
nor in Jerusalem. 22 You Samaritans worship what you do not know; we
worship what we do know, for salvation is from the Jews. 23 Yet a time is
coming and has now come when the true worshipers will worship the
Father in spirit and truth, for they are the kind of worshipers the Father
seeks. 24 God is spirit, and his worshipers must worship in spirit and in
truth." 25 The woman said, "I know that Messiah" (called Christ) "is
coming. When he comes, he will explain everything to us." 26 Then Jesus
declared, "I who speak to you am he." 27 Just then his disciples returned

and were surprised to find him talking with a woman. But no one asked,
"What do you want?" or "Why are you talking with her?" 28 Then, leaving
her water jar, the woman went back to the town and said to the people, 29
"Come, see a man who told me everything I ever did. Could this be the
Christ?" 30 They came out of the town and made their way toward him. 31
Meanwhile his disciples urged him, "Rabbi, eat something." 32 But he said
to them, "I have food to eat that you know nothing about." 33 Then his
disciples said to each other, "Could someone have brought him food?" 34
"My food," said Jesus, "is to do the will of him who sent me and to finish
his work. 35 Do you not say, `Four months more and then the harvest'? I
tell you, open your eyes and look at the fields! They are ripe for harvest. 36
Even now the reaper draws his wages, even now he harvests the crop for
eternal life, so that the sower and the reaper may be glad together. 37 Thus
the saying `One sows and another reaps' is true. 38 I sent you to reap what
you have not worked for. Others have done the hard work, and you have
reaped the benefits of their labor." 39 Many of the Samaritans from that
town believed in him because of the woman's testimony, "He told me
everything I ever did." 40 So when the Samaritans came to him, they urged
him to stay with them, and he stayed two days. 41 And because of his
words many more became believers. 42 They said to the woman, "We no
longer believe just because of what you said; now we have heard for
ourselves, and we know that this man really is the Savior of the world."

He Shared the Word with Anyone

My uncle told a story about witnessing to a used car salesman. He shared his faith with him off and on, and finally as they were discussing eternity one day, the salesman said he didn't care if he went to heaven because he just wanted to go wherever his friends were going. My uncle, fed-up with this man's ignorant apathy, replied, "Well, go to hell then."

Needless to say this wasn't the reaction the salesman expected and he was taken back by this clergy's gutsy response. My uncle was willing to share his faith with anyone—even to throw his "pearl to the swine" (Matthew 7:6) for the hope of this man's salvation. One commentator advised: "So, too, there are men so dull, imbruted and senseless, as to reject the pearls of truth."[32]

John chapter four is the textual home of the renowned “living water” account where Jesus spoke with the "woman at the well." He preached an evangelistic message to her wrapped around the metaphor, “living water". After He asked her to give Him some (physical) water from the well, He said He could offer her (spiritual) "living" water that would make it so she would never thirst again. In other words, her spiritual emptiness could be completely filled by receiving His life-quenching drink.

"Jesus did not concern Himself with any of these potential barriers as He poured truth into her parched soul."

Jesus communicated this truth to her in several different ways. First, He addressed her in public. Now I know this doesn't sound terribly profound, but in verse 9, the text informs the reader that Jews did not commonly associate with Samaritans. Nor did men speak to women in public places[33] and few spoke with women of her stature (divorcee five times and now living with a man).[34] Craig Keener adds that, "even her water vessel was considered unclean for Jewish drinking." [35] Jesus did not concern Himself with any of these potential barriers as He poured truth into her parched soul. He was in no way prejudiced regarding whom He spoke to or where they'd be seen conversing.

This is a vital lesson for Christians to learn as some feel they cannot associate with certain people or be in questionable places since the Bible has exhorted them to "abstain from the *appearance* of evil". This is clearly not what this passage is teaching, for if it were, Jesus Himself would be guilty of sin since He was a "friend of sinners" (Matthew 11:19; Luke 7:34) and likely appeared to be sinning since He was often in evil environs. Further, a literal English rendering of the Greek here in 1 Thessalonians 5:22 is that we must "avoid every form of evil"--a personal challenge to be pure in a world that is anything but.

We must be willing to associate with anyone for the sake of their souls, since they are potential disciples of Jesus Christ. The Apostle Paul affirmed the openness of the Gospel when He wrote to the Galatians, "There is neither Jew nor Greek, slave nor free, male nor female, for you are all one in Christ Jesus" (3:28). He also advised the Corinthians similarly in regard to his philosophy of ministry, "To the weak I became weak, to win the weak. I have become all things to all men so that by all possible means I might save some" (9:22).

Jesus' own brother, James, exhorted: "as believers in our glorious Lord Jesus Christ, don't show favoritism" (James 2:1). Verse 9 goes even deeper, claiming that when believers show favoritism, they sin and are convicted by the law." God has made His message of grace available to all people and no one should deny it to anyone else. Remember, "all have sinned and fallen short of the glory of God" (Romans 3:23).

Jesus shared the Word with anyone.

Thanks to Peter Mason 03-12-2007

THESE "ON-FIRE CHRISTIANS" SURE COME IN HANDY AT THESE BARBECUES

He Made it Memorable

A second point worthy of notice in Jesus' witness to the Samaritan woman was the implementation of another metaphorical hook like He used with Nicodemus. He caught her mind's eye by creating the word picture: "living water." This captivated her imagination and made her curious to find out what He meant by this new concept. Of course, the text is clear that He was talking about satisfying her spiritual thirst, but observe that this metaphor fit the context perfectly and therefore became unforgettable. Chances are that she and Nicodemus had Jesus' word pictures, "living water" and "born again" burned into their memories for the rest of their lives.

Great teachers are able to impact their listeners in such a way that they are enabled to recall much of what they have been taught for great lengths of time. The truth is, they may never forget such influence and wisdom.

The context of this event alone was another cause for a memorable occasion. Added to this was Jesus' revelation of the sordid details of her life's story. With all of these things combined, how could anyone in her sandals ever forget the experience and the lessons learned from this Rabbi from Nazareth?

Jesus made it memorable.

Thanks to David Lundahl (See Mark 10:21) 09-15-2006

YOU SAID TAKE UP LACROSSE AND FOLLOW YOU
... NOW WHAT?

He Testified About God

Jesus was not just declaring possession of living water, but that He Himself was the Living Water! His bold claim must have made this water-drawer even more curious as to who He truly was. Successfully, He hooked her attention further with these bizarre statements of His deity, His revelation of His true identity—God in the flesh. He used his personal testimony to communicate His message of Good News.

Of course, any authentic Christian testimony would be very different from His, since it would be entirely human and could not rightly claim Godhood. Though we cannot claim divinity or offer ourselves as living water, we can still use such word pictures or similar metaphors because Jesus, the living water, has quenched the spiritual thirst of all who have called on His name in trusting faith. He has quenched the thirst that parched the soul of every pre-believer before meeting Him, with the drink of Himself, resulting in peace and satisfaction for the present time, and eternal life for the future. This changed life experience is always something that can be shared with even the worst skeptic, particularly since no one can argue away the validity of another's personal experience.

The Bible affirms the incredible power of personal testimony, acknowledging it to be a victorious weapon of spiritual warfare. The apostle John wrote of the defeat of the devil in Revelation 12:11 by the testimony of the saints, "They overcame him by the blood of the Lamb and by the *word of their testimony*; they did not love their lives so much as to shrink from death."

How important it is for believers to have something ready to say about their personal experience with Jesus. The apostle Peter exhorted the need for readiness also, "But in your hearts set apart Christ as Lord. Always be prepared to give an answer to everyone who asks you to give the reason for the hope that you have" (1 Peter 3:15).

Jesus testified about God.

REVERENDFUN.COM COPYRIGHT GG, INC
Thanks to John Tomlin
JUST ... A CLOSER WALK WITH ME ...

He Saves

Being typical college students, we headed off campus one night to find something "good" to eat, since we considered the cafeteria food to be well, let's just say, "something less than fit for human consumption." Looking back I would have to say that the food at Moody Bible Institute was actually pretty good, but at that time, after sampling the same menu week after week, it had its limitations as to the satisfaction of our teenage desires and expectations.

We headed to the south side of downtown Chicago which was the home of several discos that had restaurants fronting them, not to mention streets full of drug pushers, pimps and ladies of the night, (talk about an education for a small town boy). Moody students were not allowed to attend clubs and neither did we want to, but the steak and potatoes in those diners was cheap, tasty and plentiful! What more could three young hungry men want?

Just a few buildings before reaching our dining haven, we were approached by a very large and aggressive, black drug-pusher looking to unload some of his weed.

"Jesus is cool, but He's bad for the business!"

"You dudes want to buy some smoke?" He asked, or rather, demanded of us three smaller, white, naive teens.

I replied bravely and yet cautiously, "We're not into that stuff."

Then immediately, before Jim or I could stop him, little Chaz replied, "Hey man, we're into Jesus, you got to try Jesus!"

We were nervous about his response, but the giant-sized drug-pusher calmly replied, "Well, Jesus is cool, but he's bad for the business!" He casually walked off as if we were people he respected. The very least that can be said about this experience is that this pusher completely changed his demeanor when the name of Jesus was pronounced!

The precious name of Jesus! What a name. It casts out fears and it casts out demons! It causes knees to bend and hearts to bow. It is the code word that enables entrance into the most desired of locations—heaven, the home of God.

"Jesus... the code word that enables entrance into the most desired of locations..."

When the woman at the well asked where she could get the living water, Jesus answered her specifically and without hesitation, "Everyone who drinks this water will be thirsty again but whoever drinks the water I give him, will never thirst." (v. 13) It is significant to note, as in the case with Nicodemus, that it was the creator of the universe (John 4:1-4) who answered her question. The water Jesus offered, not only was to come from Him the God/man (God in the flesh, John 17:22), but boasted eternal satisfaction (John 14:27) and eternal life (John 3:16) --a probing truth and certain solution to what people really need. We ought to think and pray carefully about the power and Lordship of Christ and be thoroughly convinced of it ourselves. It is at this point that sharing Jesus becomes, dare I say, "natural."

If lost souls are to know Him, they must meet Him. If they are to meet Him, we who know Him already must introduce them!

Verse 39 reveals that the woman did just that--she offered Jesus to anyone who would listen. The end result was that, "Many believed in Him because of the woman's testimony."

Jesus saves.

REVERENDFUN.COM COPYRIGHT GG, INC
Thanks to Roland Mathijssen (See Exodus 24:12)
03-24-2000

THOU SHALT MAKE BACKUPS

He Knew His Audience

Another amazing characteristic of Jesus was His uncanny ability to know the details of people‘s lives. He knew about the woman's situation before she told Him anything about herself. He charged in verse 16, "Go call your husband." She replied, "I have no husband". Then He asserted, "You are right to say you have no husband" and went on to explain her marital status precisely. Jesus was very well informed about her life. Granted He was the God-man, but He emptied Himself of much of His Godhood when He took on human form (Philippians 2:6-8) even to the extent that He did not know when He would return to collect His own (Mark 13:32).

The Gospels describe at least two other occasions where Jesus had divine insight. The texts say that Jesus addressed the disciples (Luke 9:47) and the Pharisees (Matthew 9:3) because He knew what they were thinking: "Jesus knowing their thoughts…"

Jesus promised His disciples that they would have similar speaking ability to His because He would give them the opportune words when facing persecution: "For I will give you words and wisdom that none of your adversaries will be able to resist or contradict" (Luke 21:15). They would also recall His teachings as needed when His Father sent them the Counselor, the Holy Spirit, whose ministry would be to “teach” them “all things” and “remind” them “of everything” He had said (John 14:26).

I have experienced this very truth often when I have preached, taught and counseled. The Holy Spirit has faithfully brought to my mind appropriate verses or

Biblical stories for the occasion that I certainly hadn't planned on. These sudden truths were often what ministered most to the folks I was addressing. I have even found myself doing what Erwin Lutzer admitted to when teaching--pausing to jot down Holy Spirit induced ideas so not to forget them for use on future occasions.[36]

The believers in Acts 2 were descended upon by the Holy Spirit while they were together (most likely worshiping) during the feast of Pentecost and miraculously were enabled to communicate to the Jews and others from all over the world in their native languages. For the first time, these foreigners heard the Good News, and understood it so clearly that they could not deny its necessity. The end result was that three thousand of them responded to its truth (vs. 41).

When Peter had the extraordinary opportunity to address this Pentecostal group he unquestionably spoke by the Spirit's power and leading in conjunction with his own Israeli heritage and upbringing. This resulted in a thorough and relatable knowledge of Jewish history and culture. Those in attendance that day listened respectfully for they recognized his God-given authority. In other words, he was not only led by the Spirit to preach and inform on that occasion, but had been prepped by the Spirit through much of his life to be intellectually available for God's use at that specific moment.

There have been occasions when I have preached a sermon and was encouragingly informed by a parishioner that God had spoken to them—but not through my words! Rather, He spoke by His Spirit to their hearts directly. You know something? I'm okay with that. The way I figure it is that if God wants to speak to someone about something other than the thesis I prepared, fantastic! I just want to be used by Him, it really doesn't matter how. He informed Isaiah the prophet, "My thoughts are not your thoughts, neither are your ways my ways,' declares the LORD. 9 'As the heavens are higher than the earth, so are my ways higher than your ways and my thoughts than your thoughts'" (Isaiah 55:8-9).

In addition to the Holy Spirit's counsel, there is the Holy Spirit's ministry of gift distribution (Romans 12:6-8; 1 Corinthians 12:11). Some may have received from the Holy Spirit one or more of the gifts of knowledge, wisdom, discernment and prophecy (1 Corinthians 12:7-11) to better enable them to minister to people's spiritual needs.

An effective communicator should, at the very least, take time to learn about those to whom he wishes to minister. Haddon Robinson acknowledged this necessity when he wrote that a preacher's lack of involvement in the lives of those he is trying to teach creates a rift in his ability to communicate. He offers the following familiar statement from a disgruntled church member, "The trouble is that God is like the minister: we don't see him during the week, and we don't understand him on Sunday."[37]

"...we will listen Sunday after Sunday to a pastor who invests time in us and shows he cares about us, even if he is the poorest preacher around."

If we do not know a preacher or special speaker, we really don't have a reason to trust him and are unlikely to think of this person as our teacher or leader. However, we will listen Sunday after Sunday to a pastor who invests time in us and shows he cares about us, even if he is the poorest preacher around. Just as missionaries learn to understand a culture and adopt many of the practices of that culture in order to minister to its people, so effective communicators need to connect with and understand their audiences, congregations and students.

Jesus' knowledge of the woman's experience prompted her astute response, “Sir, I can see that you are a prophet." Because He knew about her, she was enabled to know about Him.

Jesus knew His audience.

He Shared Spiritual Truth

In verse eighteen, we find that Jesus affirmed the woman's response to Him with the statement, "the information that you've told me is quite true." As we learned with Nicodemus, affirmation is an important part of establishing and maintaining a relationship. So, too, is speaking truth, as we observe that Jesus used the word five times in His conversation with her. This replication reveals that He again used repetition and review as an integral part of His interaction with the woman at the well.

When I was sixteen years old, I moved to a new high school in another community and attended youth group at a new church. I made some good friends and grew steadily in my faith. No doubt the most significant godly influencer in my life at that time was the youth pastor. Doug took me under his wing as a "Timothy" and spent a great deal of time with me--modeling Christ-like behavior, offering Biblical advice, inviting me to his home for fellowship and even creating fun opportunities for me and the other teens.

This type of mentoring was an effective way to infuse Biblical truth into my thick teenage boy skull. Church services and Sunday school classes seemed to me to have their rough spots, but being a pad-a-won (apprentice) was a splendid experience for spiritual growth.

In verse 23, the Lord said, "the time is coming when the true worshippers will worship the Father in spirit and in truth, for they are the kind of worshippers the Father seeks." This was an offer of spiritual truth directly to the woman, without a physical truth introducing it as Jesus had often done. Spiritual insight is normally directed at believers and the average Joe is not commonly privy to such information. Even believers are prone to think about the physical world and its concerns all too often, which the Apostle Paul coined as, "the affairs of this world" (1 Corinthians 7:32-33).

People need to hear spiritual insight in order to be changed by it, whether it is from the Word of God, the Holy Spirit, or from a preacher or teacher (Romans 10:14-15).

Jesus shared spiritual truth.

He Spoke with Authority

In verse 26, it can be observed that Jesus spoke to the woman with authority by replying, "I who speak to you am He." Referring to her preceding statement that the Messiah would teach them all things when He came (v. 25), He clearly called Himself the Messiah.[38] Obviously, there is only one Christ (Hebrews 1:2-6; John 3:16), but Christians can speak with authority since they belong to Him (Ephesians 2:10), are His children (John 3:1-3), His heirs (Titus 3:7), His representatives (2 Corinthians 5:20) and commissioned by Him to do so (Matthew 18:19-20).

It has been my experience, that when speakers address an audience with authority, they command more attention. When preaching or teaching what the Word of God actually says, and interpreting and explaining what it actually means, one is speaking the very words of God, and in that sense has or relates God's authority. The Apostle Peter affirmed this when he exhorted the church about the use of spiritual gifts, and preaching in particular, "If anyone speaks, he should do it as one speaking the very words of God."[39]

In Mark's Gospel, when Jesus taught at the synagogue in Capernaum, He is said to have taught, "as one who had authority" (v. 22). Yet in Luke's Gospel in this instance it reads that His "message had authority" (v. 32). My guess is that both He and His message had authority, but whatever the result of this potential Synoptic problem,[40] it is clear that His presentation was authoritative and powerful, beyond what the people were used to hearing.

Later in verse 35 after discussing His priorities with the disciples who had been concerned about food for their bodies, Jesus exhorted them to look for food for the soul and "open" their "eyes" and "look at the fields! They are ripe for harvest" (v. 35). He wanted them to understand how important it was to reap souls for the kingdom of God and that this conversation about spiritual water was far superior to the sustenance that physical food would provide. In fact, His nourishment came from doing the will of God (v. 34). He had to be commanding in His reply in order for them to comprehend the weight of human need and depravity.

Jesus spoke with authority.

WHAT HAPPENS TO SHEEP IF THEIR SHEPHERD IS ONE OF THOSE "CRYING WOLF" TYPES

He was Passionate about Making Disciples

Vance Havner was an itinerant American evangelist who grew up with a Bible in one hand and a bird book in the other. He loved seeing God's works and doing God's work. He often preached about the ills of a busy society that doesn't leave time for reflection and recreation in God's creation. He was full of wit and passion. I was privileged to hear him speak years ago as an old man who connected very well with this young man.

Havner wrote of his zeal for the work of God at a unusually young age;

> I never knew the day when I did not feel that I should preach and write. I memorized Bible portions, made little Sunday School talks, and sent my first sermon to our small town newspaper when I was nine.
>
> When I was ten… I was baptized in the South Fork River and a year later I asked the church to license me to preach. I began with a talk at the First Baptist Church of Hickory, twelve miles from my home… Dad and I went over in an early Ford with thirty horsepower—twenty of them dead. I stood on a chair and spoke while the pastor of the church stood on one side and the state evangelist stood on the other: like Aaron and Hur holding up the hands of Moses.[41]

I get so excited when I hear of youth who are passionate to serve God! They often accomplish more in their youth alone, than many older saints do in a lifetime! Remember Jesus only served actively for three and one half years and was about thirty-three years old when He left this earth! Thank God for those delightful servants like Havner who serve their whole lives for Christ!

Apparently Jesus was so passionate about ministry, He thought more highly of spiritual things than physical things. Consequently, He felt that food was not all that necessary, particularly when He had an opportunity to meet the deepest spiritual need of individuals. Verse 34 quotes Him as replying to the disciples, "My food ... is to do the will of Him who sent Me." He was ardent about the Father's will and work. The greatest concern and desire of the Christian communicator should be the same.

God's primary will for His spokesmen is that they obey Him and follow His calling for their lives. This is a spiritual act of faith, resulting in a satisfied spiritual, emotional and physical condition. Further, Jesus gave the Great Commission (Matthew 28:19-20) to all who follow Him, to be His disciples and to make disciples. Therefore, it should be the primary focus of all preaching and teaching so that people become more like Christ. This is indeed our greatest spiritual need.

Jesus was passionate about making disciples.

He Expected Results

Children from a Catholic elementary school wrote the following humorous but real answers in a general Bible test:

1. Samson slayed the Philistines with the axe of the apostles.
2. Moses went up to Mount Cyanide to get the 10 Commandments.
3. The first commandments was when Eve told Adam to eat the apple.
4. The seventh commandment was, "Thou shalt not admit adultery."
5. Moses died before he ever reached Canada.
6. Joshua fought the battle of Geritol.
7. The greatest miracle in the Bible is when Joshua told his son to stand still and he obeyed him.
8. Solomon had 300 wives and 700 porcupines.
9. When the 3 wise guys from east side arrived they found Jesus.

While most exams and tests yield less humorous results, their design is typically to aid in learning retention and measure students' progress. The result of good teaching should be reflected in the grades of the students.

"The Word of God is either going to spur people on to maturity, or stir them up to mutiny."

Effective preaching should have measurable results too. As stated earlier about Paul, wherever he preached and taught, they either responded or retaliated. It is paramount that Christian speakers realize that the Word of God is either going to spur people on to maturity or stir them up to mutiny.

Verse 39 reveals that many of the Samaritans from that town believed in Jesus because of the woman's testimony. She shared with them His knowledge and insight and its effect on her, and it had an effect on them--multiplication. This is the same concept Paul later told Timothy about, training faithful men who would become able to train others (2 Timothy 2:2).

When Jesus started His ministry He enjoyed favor from His listeners, "everyone praised Him" (Luke 4:15). Yet when He spoke to the people in His hometown synagogue in Nazareth, He experienced immediate persecution (they rioted and attempted to kill Him, Luke 4:16-31).

Results should be expected by disciples who exercise their faith in Christ. Jesus not only modeled this, but taught it. John 14:12-14 records His words, "I tell you the truth, anyone who has faith in me will do what I have been doing. He will do even greater things than these, because I am going to the Father. 13 And *I will do whatever you ask in my name*, so that the Son may bring glory to the Father. 14 You may ask me for anything in my name, and I will do it." Committed Christian leaders need to pray with anticipation and preach with expectation.

Jesus expected results.

REVERENDFUN.COM COPYRIGHT GCI, INC

MY NEW BUSINESS CARDS ARE BLANK UNTIL YOU HAVE FAITH THAT THE INFORMATION WILL APPEAR

He Selected Words Carefully

I remember a time when I had to address an issue with a church that was a partner with our ministry. I carefully wrote a letter that I thought was compassionate and clear and expected the pastor and leaders of the church to fully understand our position. I could not have been any further from the truth.

A short while later, I received a letter from the pastor threatening to pull his church out of our ministry because of the concerns I had expressed in my letter. I wrote back again trying to clarify my statements, but that was to no avail as I later realized when I read the subsequent reply.

Finally, we had a face-to-face meeting on the subject and the issue was resolved in less than an hour! Misunderstandings were the cause of the rift between us. As a result, a couple days later I had an epiphany--I realized none of this mess would ever have happened, had I simply made a phone call or personal visit instead of sending out a letter. It was so easy for the other party to misunderstand me since I was unable to find the right words to communicate properly.

If the others could have seen my facial expressions or body movements, and heard the tone of my voice, they would have empathized with me. Instead, my written words had apparently not been chosen carefully enough to reflect the real concerns I had hoped to express.

Words can be astonishingly powerful and may even move people to action. Recall that Jesus hooked Nicodemus and the Samaritan woman with word pictures, in each case--just two words! Verse 41 says that "because of His word… many more became believers."

When planning to communicate in some way, we ought to take time to pray and think about and plan our words. We must use our imagination and prepare words thoughtfully. It is essential to stimulate the thinking and reflection of the people with whom we wish to connect. They should be challenged and encouraged to think thoroughly and carefully. If they don't think, they won't discover--maybe they'll even miss out on something specific from God.

Jesus selected words carefully.

REVERENDFUN.COM COPYRIGHT GCI, INC
(See Exodus 20:1-21)
12-13-1999
WE ARE GOING TO FOCUS THE SERMON AGAIN THIS WEEK ON THE MOST IMPORTANT COMMANDMENT ... THOU SHALT NOT KILL

Starting Out

Jesus Begins His Earthly Ministry

Matthew 4

17 From that time on Jesus began to preach, "Repent, for the kingdom of heaven is near."

Mark 1

14 After John was put in prison, Jesus went into Galilee, proclaiming the good news of God. 15 "The time has come," he said. "The kingdom of God is near. Repent and believe the good news!"

Luke 4

14 Jesus returned to Galilee in the power of the Spirit, and news about him spread through the whole countryside. 15 He taught in their synagogues, and everyone praised him.

He Relied on the Holy Spirit

After Jesus had interacted with the Samaritan woman, He traveled another thirty miles[42] to Galilee to preach (according to Matthew's Gospel) and teach (Luke's Gospel) in their synagogues. Synagogues were Jewish places of instruction, much like school buildings today. They also served as community halls and courthouses for religious and criminal cases and were the place that alms were collected for the poor.[43] Jesus went to the synagogue because His people congregated there. What's more, they enjoyed gathering for the reading and exposition of the Scriptures. It was the perfect place for Him to preach and teach.

"Supernatural power is far more convincing and convicting than carefully crafted words or stories."

Luke's account of this event included the observation of Jesus' return in the "power of the Spirit" (4:14). There is no question Christian communicators are going to be far more effective with the Holy Spirit behind them, or should I say, *ahead* of them, and working through them. Supernatural power is far more convincing and convicting than carefully crafted words or stories. However, the Holy Spirit uses words too (Luke 12:11-12)!

There are at least three things Jesus taught His disciples that the Holy Spirit would do for them after He left: First, **they would receive wisdom and insight from the Holy Spirit;** "But the Counselor, the Holy Spirit, whom the Father will send in my name, will teach you all things and will remind you of everything I have said to you" (John 14:26).

Additionally, Jesus said **they would be enabled to accomplish what He had done and more**; "I tell you the truth, anyone who has faith in me will do what I have been doing. He will do even greater things than these, because I am going to the Father" (John 14:12).

Thirdly, **Christ's disciples are given words to speak in times of persecution and defense of their faith**; "Do not worry about how you will defend yourselves or what you will say, 12 for the Holy Spirit will teach you at that time what you should say" (Luke 12:11-12).

"The Christian minister possesses a remarkable partner in ministry, a secret weapon so to speak--the Holy Spirit."

The Christian minister possesses a remarkable partner in ministry, a secret weapon so to speak--the Holy Spirit. He is an available and powerful resource for any believer who seeks and serves God!

The most significant Bible verse in ministry for me in recent years has been John 15:5. It discloses Jesus as the source of any real ministry. He said, "I am the vine; you are the branches. If a man remains in me and I in him, he will bear much fruit; apart from me you can do nothing."

Did you catch that last part? **"Apart from Me, you can do NOTHING!"** Nothing in the Greek means exactly that. There is nothing of any eternal value that we can do. Nothing beneficial to the Kingdom of God and nothing that brings honor and glory to our Lord and

Savior Jesus Christ, apart from following Him! Oh how we need Him and His Spirit in our lives and our service!

Are you remaining or abiding in Jesus? Are you relying on power from heaven? Are you doing something for God, or *nothing* for Him?

The path to power in the Spirit is simple, really. All we need to do is confess our sins and ask God to fill us with His Spirit and use us in His service. Ephesians 5 explains it best:

> Do not get drunk on wine, which leads to debauchery. Instead, be filled with the Spirit. 19 Speak to one another with psalms, hymns and spiritual songs. Sing and make music in your heart to the Lord, 20 always giving thanks to God the Father for everything, in the name of our Lord Jesus Christ. 21 Submit to one another out of reverence for Christ.

An attitude of praise, thankfulness, submission and reverence is what is needed to be filled with and led by the Spirit of God. This was true of Jesus and it ought to be true of us.

Jesus relied on the Holy Spirit.

He Had a Good Reputation

My father in law has been a pastor in Maine for the greater part of his life and is now retired. It never ceases to impress me how many people know Whit and are pleased to see him wherever he goes, whether at a ball game or at the mall. His reputation for integrity and Christ-centeredness have made him a friend they can trust and respect. I can say the same for my mother-in-law (even though I have often laughed at the occasional mother-in-law joke… about other people's in-laws of course).

I have also listened to former parishioners and non-parishioners alike sing the accolades of my Reverend Uncle Fred and my Reverend Uncle Chris and their wives for their selfless and caring pastoral ministries among them. They are men and women of godly character and integrity—this is what made them great and resulted in the honorable reputations that followed.

Of course one doesn't have to be clergy to serve the Lord with a whole and pure heart in order to make it into God's Hall of Fame. Two of many such examples in my life are my adopted southern parents, Durwood and Mary. "Durd" or "the gummy worm man" as my children used to call him, is a Retired Master Chief from the U.S. Navy and retiree from the local power company. And Mary is a homemaker and powerfully good cook. They have given of themselves time and time again to the Lord's service.

Then of course there is my mother and many family members, particularly my Aunt Glenda and Uncle

Loran who have faithfully supported me and the seminary where I teach through prayer and financial gifts.

There are so many more people I could mention who have impeccable standing among their peers for Christ because of their godly character and love. I expect God has placed similar people in your life. Why not take a few moments to let them know how God has blessed you through them?

Of further note in these passages is that at the start of Jesus' ministry, "everyone praised Him" (Luke 4:15). Jesus was preaching truth and meeting the physical and spiritual needs of those around Him and the resulting consequence was their overwhelming appreciation and support for Him. People are mostly kind and thankful toward others who make personal sacrifices for them. This should be a characteristic of all believers and is extra helpful to a teacher and leader.

When the Apostle Paul listed necessary qualifications for pastors and elders in First Timothy chapter 3, he had in mind the idea of earning respect in ministry. While one of these criteria was the ability to teach skillfully (v. 2), another was to "have a good reputation with outsiders" (v. 7), and still another was to be "respectable" (v. 2). Also, the deacons were to be "men worthy of respect" (v. 8), and "be tested; and then if there is nothing against them, let them serve…" (v. 10).

Usually when a church has had division and loss of members, or a business meeting or a staff relationship has gone awry, it is the result of inadequate leadership or communication at some level or another. It is too bad we don't place more emphasis on character building and righteousness when we train leaders for our churches.

If these qualities that Paul gave Timothy are important to God, then they certainly should be for Christian leaders today--and a good reputation will follow.

Jesus had a good reputation.

DON'T HEAL ME ... I'VE GOT GREAT DISABILITY

The Truth Hurts

Jesus is Rejected in His Hometown

Luke 4

16 He went to Nazareth, where he had been brought up, and on the
Sabbath day he went into the synagogue, as was his custom. And he stood
up to read. 17 The scroll of the prophet Isaiah was handed to him.
Unrolling it, he found the place where it is written: 18 "The Spirit of the
Lord is on me, because he has anointed me to preach good news to the
poor. He has sent me to proclaim freedom for the prisoners and recovery
of sight for the blind, to release the oppressed, 19 to proclaim the year of
the Lord's favor." 20 Then he rolled up the scroll, gave it back to the
attendant and sat down. The eyes of everyone in the synagogue were
fastened on him, 21 and he began by saying to them, "Today this scripture
is fulfilled in your hearing." 22 All spoke well of him and were amazed at
the gracious words that came from his lips. "Isn't this Joseph's son?" they
asked. 23 Jesus said to them, "Surely you will quote this proverb to me:
`Physician, heal yourself! Do here in your hometown what we have heard
that you did in Capernaum.'" 24 "I tell you the truth," he continued, "no
prophet is accepted in his hometown. 25 I assure you that there were many
widows in Israel in Elijah's time, when the sky was shut for three and a half
years and there was a severe famine throughout the land. 26 Yet Elijah was
not sent to any of them, but to a widow in Zarephath in the region of
Sidon. 27 And there were many in Israel with leprosy in the time of Elisha
the prophet, yet not one of them was cleansed--only Naaman the Syrian."
28 All the people in the synagogue were furious when they heard this. 29
They got up, drove him out of the town, and took him to the brow of the
hill on which the town was built, in order to throw him down the cliff. 30
But he walked right through the crowd and went on his way. 31 Then he
went down to Capernaum, a town in Galilee, and on the Sabbath began to
teach the people.

He Read the Scriptures Publicly

Jesus returned to the place where He had grown up, and, on the Sabbath, dared teach in the synagogue. Luke is the only writer who mentions this event and states that He went to this place of Biblical education (synagogue) as was His practice ("custom" v. 16). After Jesus got up to read the pre-selected passage from the scroll of Isaiah, He told them the prophecy was fulfilled in Him that very day. He clarified that He was the promised Messiah in the flesh. Later, the people became "furious" and "drove Him out of town," and even tried to "throw Him down the cliff" (v. 29).

No doubt Jesus knew that all this would happen when He read the prophecy about Himself in the synagogue, but He did it anyway, because the reading of the Word of God and its proper interpretation were a priority for Him, as was the announcement of His deity.

When speaking or teaching, Jesus often quoted the Old Testament books, which were the Scriptures of His day. These same "Scriptures" Paul quoted (Acts 17:2, 11; Romans 1:2, 15:4; 1 Corinthians 15:3-4; and 2 Timothy 3:15) as did Peter (Acts 2:16-40; 2 Peter 3:16) and Apollos (Acts 18:24, 28).

Some of the passages Jesus cited were: the creation account (Mark 10:6-8); Abel's murder (Luke 11:51); Noah and the great flood (Luke 17:26-27); Sodom and Gomorrah and Lot and his disobedient wife (Luke 17:28-32); Moses and the burning bush (Luke 20:37); Moses and the manna from heaven (John 6:31); Moses and the bronze serpent (John 3:14); David and the consecrated bread (Matthew 12:3-4); Solomon and the queen of Sheba (Matthew 12:42); Elijah and the widow and the famine (Luke 4:25-36); Naaman, the Syrian's, cleansing from leprosy (Luke 4:27); Zechariah's murder (Luke 11:51); Daniel's prophecy of the Antichrist (Matthew 24:15); Jonah and the big fish (Matthew 12:40; 16:4); and Jonah's preaching and Nineveh's repentance (Luke 11:30 and Matthew 12:41).

Hebrews 4:12 informs us of the importance of God's Word: "the word of God is living and active. Sharper than any double-edged sword, it penetrates even to dividing soul and spirit, joints and marrow; it judges the thoughts and attitudes of the heart."

Psalm 119 further teaches us that there are at least two things we can know and two things we can keep from our experience with the Scriptures; **we can know God** (vv. 20, 26, 88, 90, 102, 136, 142, 151, 152, 156, 159, 160) and **we can know God's will** (vv. 30, 66, 98-100, 105, 130), and **we can keep from sinning** (vv. 9, 11, 133) and **we can keep satisfied** (vv. 14, 24, 32, 47, 50, 52, 97, 103, 127, 143, 164-166).

For those who read or hear the book of Revelation read aloud, there is also a blessing; "Blessed is the one who reads the words of this prophecy, and blessed are those who hear it and take to heart what is written in it, because the time is near."

Jesus read the Scriptures publicly.

Thanks to Dad Hengeveld (See Matthew 10:29-31) 12-02-1999

TODAY'S READING IS MATTHEW 10:30 ...
"BUT THE VERY HAIRS OF YOUR HEAD ARE ALL
... ER ... NUMBERED"

He was Faithful to His Calling and Gifts

The passage Jesus read in Isaiah 61, states something about His preaching that deserves notation. It declares that He was “anointed” by the Spirit of the Lord to “preach" good news to the poor (v. 18), “proclaim” freedom to the prisoners (v. 18), and “proclaim” the year of the Lord’s favor (v. 19). In addition to being chosen as our (once for all) atoning sacrifice for sins, Christ (whose name means "anointed")[44] was unquestionably “anointed” for a communication ministry as well!

The root for the word "anoint" in the Greek explains that He was “consecrated to the messianic office…and furnished with the necessary powers of its administration.”[45] When this word is used of Christians, it refers to the empowerment of the Holy Spirit for special tasks of ministry.[46]

I recently asked one of our professors, who has been a pastor close to thirty years, to share from his heart with my pastoral ministry class. He addressed the matter of "a call to ministry" from God and emphatically stated that if they were not compelled and driven to pastoral ministry, they had better not pursue it at all! He stressed how tough and lonely the pastoral road was to walk and that it could potentially build more stress than man is expected to manage. It does carry with it great joy and reward, but if they were not called; they had better quit while they were ahead.

As I thought about my pastoral ministry experience and that of shepherds I know, I agreed. Only those who are called and gifted for that task ought to do it. I was reminded of the great need for more emphasis and education regarding these dual necessities for ministry: calling and giftedness.

Obviously every saved believer has experienced a call to salvation through the Holy Spirit's conviction (John 16:8) and in turn has called back to Him (John 3:36; 5:24; 15:4; Acts 2:21). Additionally, every believer is to reproduce by making more disciples (those who are like their teacher) as Jesus directed in the Great Commission (Matthew 28:19-20). But there is yet another call, and this one is specific to a certain ministry or ministry task.

Many considering pastoral ministry or missions have asked about the "call to ministry" (probably because of the high level of commitment required) and how they can know if they are being called. Well, here are a few useful nuggets from Gods' Word to help with this query:

1. God's call is obvious. Matthew recounts the first calling by our Lord (Ch. 4:18-22). When He approached Peter and Andrew, he spoke to them loudly and clearly (loudly because they were in their boat off-shore casting their nets and may have had difficulty hearing someone on shore, and clearly, because they understood and obeyed)! Like my pastor friend said, one should be compelled to ministry by an obvious call from God.

2. God will call when you are giving your best effort in your present situation. Acts 9 records that this was true with the conversion of Saul, where Jesus called him to apostolic service. We find that Paul was striving to serve

> *"Paul was busy serving God and Jesus blind-sided him by blinding him."*

God to the best of his ability and power (partly by eliminating what he saw as the Christian cult). Jesus knew Paul's real passion was to please God, so He stopped him on his way to Damascus and confronted him, calling him to preach and suffer for His sake. Paul was busy serving God and Jesus blind-sided him by blinding him. The call could not have been any more convincing!

3. God will call in His time. I am certain that both Paul and Ananias were surprised at God's timing when he called them. Saul and his companions must have been shocked at Jesus' appearance on the road in front of them in the middle of their trip. Saul lost his sight and they lost their voices. The timing was so unexpected!

Ananias questioned the Lord because of Saul's recent persecution of the saints and was probably struggling with his specific call, yet he was obedient. For us, God is full of surprises--He is far above our human state and level of understanding, "'My thoughts are not your thoughts, neither are your ways my ways,' declares the LORD. 9 'As the heavens are higher than the earth, so are my ways higher than your ways and my thoughts than your thoughts'" (Isaiah 55:8).

4. God will often call through mature believers. Ananias was informed by the Lord in a vision that Saul would be His "chosen instrument" to carry His name "before the Gentiles and their kings and before the people of Israel" (v. 15). Ananias was God's man to help Paul see with both his eyes and his soul. Proverbs 15:22 reminds us that a person with many counselors is wise and chapter 27 verse 17 says, "As iron sharpens iron, so one man sharpens another." Listen to the godly people around you, like Paul listened to Ananias.

5. God will call in worship. We find in Acts 13:2 that the Holy Spirit spoke directly to the worshiping believers about Paul and Barnabas' calling: "While they were worshiping the Lord and fasting, *the Holy Spirit said*, 'Set apart for me Barnabas and Saul for the work to which I have *called* them.'" The word worship actually means the same as service [47] and some translations use "service" in this verse in place of worship. Isn't it a bit ironic that we call our worship gatherings "worship services?" What we are really saying is that we attend service services.

The point is this; all believers are called *to minister to the Lord* (praise, prayer, offerings, etc.) and *to minister for the Lord* (discipling, caring, witnessing and so on).

6. God wants to use your gifts and skills. There are at least twenty-one gifts mentioned in five different passages of Scripture [48] and countless skill sets described throughout it. There must be something in these lists that you and I are to use for God's Kingdom work! Romans 12 (and 1 Corinthians 12-14) teaches that believers are part of a body (v. 5) possessing different gifts for each other's benefit (v. 6; 1 Corinthians 12:11). The Lord also told the Church in Corinth (Corinthians 13) that His gifts are to be motivated by and exercised in love (v. 31) and they are worthless if not so used (vv. 1-4).

Are you faithfully doing *what* God has asked you to do? Are you doing it the *way* He wants you to? Are you serving Him out of love?

Jesus was faithful to His calling and gifts.

Thanks to Dad Hengeveld 12-28-1999

FROSTY THE SNOWMAN'S CALL TO THE MINISTRY WAS SUCCESSFUL UNTIL HE ACCEPTED A CALL TO LOUISIANA

He Was Gracious

The Reverend Robert Runcie, retired Archbishop of Canterbury, wrote in his book, Seasons of the Spirit, that he once got on a train in England and discovered that all the other passengers in the car were patients at a mental institution being taken on an excursion.

A mental hospital attendant was counting the patients to be sure that they were all there: "One, two, three, four, five..." When he came to Runcie, he said, "Who are you?"

"I am the Archbishop of Canterbury," Runcie replied.

The attendant smiled and, pointing to him, continued counting,"...six, seven, eight..."[49]

The Archbishop was certainly a gracious man considering his predicament. We know this to be true of Jesus. Verse 22 reveals that even His speaking style was gracious. It reads that He spoke with "gracious words" and up to this point the people were speaking "well" of Him. They were even "amazed" at His gracious words.

The Greek word for "gracious" used here means, "goodwill, loving kindness, favor, loveliness, grace of speech."[50] In fact, the word "grace" came from an old Hebrew word that meant, "to bend, to stoop."[51] The late pastor and Bible scholar Donald Barnhouse astutely wrote, "Love that goes upward is worship; love that goes outward is affection; *love that stoops* is grace."[52]

Jesus' words were loving and kind, even though He knew the reaction to His testimony would become hateful and deadly (v. 29). Paul agreed with this behavior in his inspired letter to the Colossians, "Be wise in the way you act toward outsiders; make the most of every opportunity. 6 Let your conversation be always *full of grace*, seasoned with salt, so that you may know how to answer everyone."

Jesus was gracious.

REVERENDFUN.COM COPYRIGHT GCI, INC

Thanks to Tom Seubert (See Mark 11:15-26) 08-02-2002

NO, I DON'T APPRECIATE THE IRONY ... NOW PLEASE GET OUT

He Followed God's Plan

After His testimony, the people in Nazareth took Jesus to the brow of a hill and attempted to push Him off a cliff. I have been in Nazareth a couple of times and I can tell you there is no shortage of high cliffs there. The whole town sits on top of a very large mountain. Jesus was the Son of God, and given the fact that it wasn't time for His death, the crowd was incapable of proceeding with their lethal intentions. The text says, "But He walked right through the crowd and went on His way" (v. 30).

"Even while Satan could stir the crowd's feelings, he could not steer their fate."

Even while Satan could stir the crowd's feelings, he could not steer their fate. God's purposes always advance as He wishes. This is why Jesus walked through the crowd so easily: God had plans for Him to minister further to people before His earthly departure. Satan and all his hoards could not alter what God set out to do.

Paul affirmed this truth with the Ephesian Church when he wrote that a believer's struggle is not against people, but, "...against the powers of this dark world and against the spiritual forces of evil in the heavenly realms"(Ephesians 6:12). James reminded us by the moving of the Holy Spirit that when we submit to God and resist the devil, he will flee from us (James 4:7). Jesus taught the disciples that they would do greater things than He did (John 14:12), but they would need to pray regularly for protection from the evil one. This became apparent when He gave them the celebrated "Lord's Prayer" (or better, disciple's prayer, Matthew 6:9-13) and later prayed a very similar petition for them in the Garden of Gethsemane the night before His death, submitting His own will to the Father's (John 17:15).

When Lucifer wanted to harm Job, he had to get permission from God first (Job 1:6-12). God is still in control and continues to do miraculous things for His children. No one can interfere with a believer if he or she is living in obedience to God's will--not even Satan himself. Paul assured us of this with his letter to the Roman Church when he wrote, "What, then, shall we say in response to this? If God is for us, who can be against us?" (Romans 8:31)

In 1895, the January 24th edition of The Star-Herald newspaper recorded the following story:

> The joke is on a Caribou young man who, one evening last week after harnessing his horse, left him standing in front of the house until an overcoat could be secured.
>
> The animal was not attached to a vehicle and left the house before the young man secured the coat. It appears that the young owner of the horse had been in the habit of visiting nightly, a certain young lady living about seven miles from his home.
>
> On the night in question, the young gentleman remained at home and vainly hunted for his lost animal. About 4 a.m. the horse returned home and made his presence known to his master. The next evening the young man visited his best girl

and found that the evening before the horse had been seen near the house for a short time, but had disappeared.

Thus it was ascertained, that the horse made his usual nightly visit, but without his master.

Are you consistent like the horse was? Do you try to go where He does each day? Do you follow His will even when you don't feel His presence with you?

If you are confused about what His will is for you, here is some simple advice; it begins with a relationship with Christ (Romans 3:23; 6:23; 10:8-9) and continues through faithfulness to the instructions in God's word (2 Timothy 2:15). I always recommend to new believers or returning believers to read the "J" books in the New Testament in the following order; The Gospel of John (which reveals Jesus as God/man), 1 John (which reveals God's intense love for His children) and James (which provides practical Christian living instruction). It is also helpful to read Ephesians 5 where we are exhorted to "find out what pleases the Lord" (vs. 10) and "understand what the Lord's will is" (vs. 17). If you want God's will--know God's word. Jesus did.

He followed God's plan.

REVERENDFUN.COM COPYRIGHT GCI, INC

Thanks to John Fenn (See John 19:17-37) 11-11-1999

UMMM JESUS, ARE YOU SURE YOU DON'T WANT TO BE A FIREMAN OR PHARAOH WHEN YOU GROW UP? ... 'CRUCIFIED, DEAD AND BURIED' IS A BIT TOO SPOOKY FOR THE OTHER KIDS

Absolute Authority
Jesus is Accepted at Capernaum

Mark 1

21 They went to Capernaum, and when the Sabbath came, Jesus went into the synagogue and began to teach. 22 The people were amazed at his teaching, because he taught them as one who had authority, not as the teachers of the law. 23 Just then a man in their synagogue who was possessed by an evil spirit cried out, 24 "What do you want with us, Jesus of Nazareth? Have you come to destroy us? I know who you are--the Holy One of God!" 25 "Be quiet!" said Jesus sternly. "Come out of him!" 26
The evil spirit shook the man violently and came out of him with a shriek.
27 The people were all so amazed that they asked each other, "What is this? A new teaching--and with authority! He even gives orders to evil spirits and they obey him." 28 News about him spread quickly over the whole region of Galilee.

Luke 4

31 Then he went down to Capernaum, a town in Galilee, and on the Sabbath began to teach the people. 32 They were amazed at his teaching, because his message had authority. 33 In the synagogue there was a man possessed by a demon, an evil spirit. He cried out at the top of his voice, 34
"Ha! What do you want with us, Jesus of Nazareth? Have you come to destroy us? I know who you are--the Holy One of God!" 35 "Be quiet!" Jesus said sternly. "Come out of him!" Then the demon threw the man down before them all and came out without injuring him. 36 All the people were amazed and said to each other, "What is this teaching? With authority and power he gives orders to evil spirits and they come out!" 37
And the news about him spread throughout the surrounding area.

He Used Spiritual Sight

It is unlikely that the Jewish people were ready that day for the event that unfolded before their eyes. Jesus, a relatively new and curious Rabbi, appeared before them to instruct them, and somewhere in the midst of His message, a demon-possessed man yelled out a testimony of who Jesus really was--the Son of God (v. 24). Whether or not those who were present knew the man was possessed, Jesus certainly did, and rectified the situation immediately by exorcising the demon. Christ had an uncanny ability to discern and perceive the spiritual world around Him.

Missionaries from Cuba tell the story of a village witch doctor who was noted for his spirituality. As strange as it may sound, he became alarmed with the immoral condition of the community in which he practiced and one day decided to go to a nearby city to seek out a better place to raise his family. While there, Vincente' got distracted by a religious bookstore and after entering it became fascinated by a "holy" book which he purchased. He took the book home with him and continued to read it. At his next séance he quoted from this new revelation, and the "Holy Bible" became a hit among his followers. Soon they had discovered Jesus and His sacrifice for their sins and received Him as their Lord!

"Jesus, of course, was even more in tune with the spiritual world; always able to distinguish, diagnose and deal with it…"

Vicente' possessed enough spiritual sight to recognize the truth when he found it. Jesus, of course, was even more in tune with the spiritual world; always able to distinguish, diagnose and deal with it properly. Christian communicators must learn to put on their spiritual glasses in order to gain a spiritual perspective. This can be achieved through constant communion with God--the divine optometrist.

Jesus used Spiritual sight.

I'M GLAD YOU'VE ARRIVED DR. GUSTAVSTEN ... YOU'LL BE PLEASED TO NOTE THAT THESE NATIVES ARE NOT NEARLY AS HARD TO DEAL WITH AS WE HAD ORIGINALLY THOUGHT

He Exercised Spiritual Authority

He couldn't do it! He couldn't say the name of Jesus! He couldn't even read his Bible, pray or experience any joy in his Christian walk.

"What is happening to me?" He asked glumly but with unshakable curiosity.

My friend had been a Christian for two years and was also attending Sunday evening services at a fringe "Health & Wealth" church, one that made even my Pentecostal brothers cringe. As I asked him about his experiences just before this strange behavior overtook him, he was eventually able to trace its beginning to one of those Sunday evenings in which he had been "slain" (which actually means murdered or slaughtered) or should I say pushed over and entranced. Whatever the case, we believed he had become oppressed by a demon or demons since he was no longer capable of fellowship with Christ.

There were three of us there to pray for him. We laid hands on him and asked God to deliver him from this oppression so that he could come back to communion with Jesus. I then commanded whatever demon(s) that might be involved in this situation to leave in Jesus' name. After saying "amen" my friend replied, "Praise Jesus." He also told us he had felt a shiver as we were praying as if something left him and the presence of the Lord filled him. For the first time in several weeks he could fellowship with his Heavenly Father! Spiritual authority was the weapon we wielded to effectively defeat the enemy's "foothold" on my friend (Ephesians 4:27).

Jesus did more than just decipher the spiritual climate in the synagogue; He did something about it. When He heard the demon shriek, He silenced him immediately and without effort! What authority! With just a few words, the demon was gone and the weary man was healed. The people witnessed Christ's authority up close and personal.

Paul taught the believers in the Church at Ephesus how to wield this kind of power by dressing with spiritual armor: the belt of truth, breastplate of righteousness, the shoes of readiness to share the Gospel, the shield of faith, the helmet of assurance and knowledge of salvation, and the sword of the Spirit, the Word of God (Ephesians 6:13-17). He added that they needed to "pray in the Spirit" and "keep on praying for all the saints" (v. 18). Through prayer, the Scriptures, obedience, assurance and truth-speaking, God's spokesperson can overturn the spiritual world just like Jesus did!

Jesus exercised Spiritual authority.

REVERENDFUN.COM COPYRIGHT GCI, INC
Thanks to Zachary J. Schertz
04-06-2007
... HE DESCENDED INTO HELL ... AND REALLY FREAKED OUT THE LOCALS

Purpose Driven

Jesus Reveals Why He Came

Matthew 4

23 Jesus went throughout Galilee, teaching in their synagogues, preaching
the good news of the kingdom, and healing every disease and sickness
among the people. 24 News about him spread all over Syria, and people
brought to him all who were ill with various diseases, those suffering severe
pain, the demon-possessed, those having seizures, and the paralyzed, and he
healed them. 25 Large crowds from Galilee, the Decapolis, Jerusalem,
Judea and the region across the Jordan followed him.

Mark 1

35 Very early in the morning, while it was still dark, Jesus got up, left the
house and went off to a solitary place, where he prayed. 36 Simon and his
companions went to look for him, 37 and when they found him, they
exclaimed: "Everyone is looking for you!" 38 Jesus replied, "Let us go
somewhere else--to the nearby villages--so I can preach there also. That is
why I have come." 39 So he traveled throughout Galilee, preaching in their
synagogues and driving out demons.

Luke 4

42 At daybreak Jesus went out to a solitary place. The people were looking
for him and when they came to where he was, they tried to keep him from
leaving them. 43 But he said, "I must preach the good news of the
kingdom of God to the other towns also, because that is why I was sent."
44 And he kept on preaching in the synagogues of Judea.

He was Committed

Henry Dempsey was the pilot for a commuter flight from Portland, Maine to Boston, Massachusetts. Shortly after take-off one day, he heard a strange noise in the back of the plane and decided to investigate it. As he neared the tail of the aircraft an air pocket bumped the jet and threw him against the back door, which to his surprise was the cause of the noise. Of even greater shock was the fact that the door flung open and he was sucked out entirely. The co-pilot instantly radioed the airport for an emergency landing and for a helicopter to begin a search for Captain Dempsey.

After they landed, they found him clinging to the ladder of the plane. Somehow he caught it and managed to hang on to it for ten minutes at 4000 feet above the ground and at a speed of 200 miles per hour! He didn't even hit the ground during landing. Several minutes were needed for the rescue workers to pry Dempsey's fingers from the aircraft. Needless to say, he was intensely committed to hanging on.

"The fact that the Son was up before the sun suggests an intense commitment to His personal communion with God."

These passages of Scripture expose Christ's priority, purpose, plan and power for ministry. His utmost priority was undoubtedly to maintain His relationship with the Father as can be seen in Mark 1:35, "Very early in the morning, while it was still dark, Jesus got up, left the house and went off to a solitary place, where He prayed." The fact that the Son was up before the sun, suggests an intense commitment to His personal communion with God. It was more important to Jesus to have spiritual rest than the obvious physical rest His body craved. He was probably the only preacher who ever truly and fully practiced what He preached.

The Lord's purpose is found in verse 38 where He exclaims, "Let us go somewhere else--to the nearby villages--so I can ***preach*** there also. That is why I have come." Jesus unmistakably informed His disciples that He came with the specific task of preaching, and according to verse 39, He carried through with it! Luke tells us that the ***content*** of His preaching was the Gospel: "I must preach the good news of the Kingdom of God," (4:43) and the ***context*** of His preaching was mainly in publicly accessible places including synagogues (where Jewish people met for Scriptural study and community events).

"Jesus' preaching came not only with grand words, but with great works."

If His purpose was to preach, His plan was to take His message to the people. In the "nearby villages" (Mark 1:38), "throughout Galilee" (Matthew 4:23; Luke 1:39), to "other towns" (Luke 4:43) and to "the synagogues of Judea" (Luke 4:44). His plan was both comprehensive and obtainable.

Jesus' preaching came not only with grand words, but with great works. Most often His communication ministry was coupled with supernatural power. He cured individuals--in both body: "healed them" (Matthew 4:24) and soul: "driving out demons" (Mark 1:39).

Jesus' passion and priority was to be in His Father's will, and the result was an incredible ministry with purpose, plan and power! This type of ministry is not restricted only to the Savior, but is available to any disciple of Jesus Christ who is willing to follow Him! He even promised His disciples that they would do greater things than He did (John 14:12).

What is it that you have to communicate? Why is it a priority that you share it? Do you have a purpose and plan to make it happen? Is your message in line with God's so that He will allow His power to accompany it?

Next time you set out to teach, preach, lead or serve, consider such questions. Countless leaders have failed because they have overlooked God's will and leading, following instead their own carefully crafted agenda. Remember, Jesus said, "Apart from Me, you can do nothing" (John 15:5b).

Jesus was committed.

God/Man at Work
Jesus Heals on the Sabbath

John 5
1 Some time later, Jesus went up to Jerusalem for a feast of the Jews. 2
Now there is in Jerusalem near the Sheep Gate a pool, which in Aramaic is
called Bethesda and which is surrounded by five covered colonnades. 3
Here a great number of disabled people used to lie--the blind, the lame, the
paralyzed. 4 From time to time an angel of the Lord would come down
and stir up the waters. The first one into the pool after each such
disturbance would be cured of whatever disease he had. 5 One who was
there had been an invalid for thirty-eight years. 6 When Jesus saw him
lying there and learned that he had been in this condition for a long time, he
asked him, "Do you want to get well?" 7 "Sir," the invalid replied, "I have
no one to help me into the pool when the water is stirred. While I am trying
to get in, someone else goes down ahead of me." 8 Then Jesus said to him,
"Get up! Pick up your mat and walk." 9 At once the man was cured; he
picked up his mat and walked. The day on which this took place was a
Sabbath, 10 and so the Jews said to the man who had been healed, "It is
the Sabbath; the law forbids you to carry your mat." 11 But he replied,
"The man who made me well said to me, `Pick up your mat and walk.'" 12
So they asked him, "Who is this fellow who told you to pick it up and
walk?" 13 The man who was healed had no idea who it was, for Jesus had
slipped away into the crowd that was there. 14 Later Jesus found him at
the temple and said to him, "See, you are well again. Stop sinning or
something worse may happen to you." 15 The man went away and told the
Jews that it was Jesus who had made him well. 16 So, because Jesus was
doing these things on the Sabbath, the Jews persecuted him. 17 Jesus said
to them, "My Father is always at his work to this very day, and I, too, am
working." 18 For this reason the Jews tried all the harder to kill him; not
only was he breaking the Sabbath, but he was even calling God his own
Father, making himself equal with God. 19 Jesus gave them this answer: "I
tell you the truth, the Son can do nothing by himself; he can do only what
he sees his Father doing, because whatever the Father does the Son also
does. 20 For the Father loves the Son and shows him all he does. Yes, to
your amazement he will show him even greater things than these. 21 For
just as the Father raises the dead and gives them life, even so the Son gives
life to whom he is pleased to give it. 22 Moreover, the Father judges no
one, but has entrusted all judgment to the Son, 23 that all may honor the

Son just as they honor the Father. He who does not honor the Son does
not honor the Father, who sent him. 24 "I tell you the truth, whoever
hears my word and believes him who sent me has eternal life and will not be
condemned; he has crossed over from death to life. 25 I tell you the truth,
a time is coming and has now come when the dead will hear the voice of
the Son of God and those who hear will live. 26 For as the Father has life
in himself, so he has granted the Son to have life in himself. 27 And he has
given him authority to judge because he is the Son of Man. 26 For as the
Father has life in himself, so he has granted the Son to have life in himself.
27 And he has given him authority to judge because he is the Son of Man.
28 "Do not be amazed at this, for a time is coming when all who are in
their graves will hear his voice 29 and come out--those who have done
good will rise to live, and those who have done evil will rise to be
condemned. 30 By myself I can do nothing; I judge only as I hear, and my
judgment is just, for I seek not to please myself but him who sent me. 31
"If I testify about myself, my testimony is not valid. 32 There is another
who testifies in my favor, and I know that his testimony about me is valid.
33 "You have sent to John and he has testified to the truth. 34 Not that I
accept human testimony; but I mention it that you may be saved. 35 John
was a lamp that burned and gave light, and you chose for a time to enjoy his
light. 36 "I have testimony weightier than that of John. For the very work
that the Father has given me to finish, and which I am doing, testifies that
the Father has sent me. 37 And the Father who sent me has himself
testified concerning me. You have never heard his voice nor seen his form,
38 nor does his word dwell in you, for you do not believe the one he sent.
39 You diligently study the Scriptures because you think that by them you
possess eternal life. These are the Scriptures that testify about me, 40 yet
you refuse to come to me to have life. 41 "I do not accept praise from
men, 42 but I know you. I know that you do not have the love of God in
your hearts. 43 I have come in my Father's name, and you do not accept
me; but if someone else comes in his own name, you will accept him. 44
How can you believe if you accept praise from one another, yet make no
effort to obtain the praise that comes from the only God? 45 "But do not
think I will accuse you before the Father. Your accuser is Moses, on whom
your hopes are set. 46 If you believed Moses, you would believe me, for he
wrote about me. 47 But since you do not believe what he wrote, how are
you going to believe what I say?"

He Was Humble

Again Jesus preached to the Jews and assorted Gentiles about who He really was and why He was there. It was an opportunity that resulted from exercising spiritual and physical power--the healing of the lame man. He told the man to pick up his mat and walk, and to the Jews that was work. They were more concerned about the work than the worker. In all their religiosity and rigor they came to fear the Law more than the Lawgiver. They completely forgot the love commands like, "Do not seek revenge or bear a grudge against one of your people, but love your neighbor as yourself. I am the LORD" (Leviticus 19:18).

The reply of the restored man is noteworthy: when He was asked who had healed him--he had "no idea who it was…" since Jesus had "slipped away into the crowd" (v. 13). This action suggests Jesus was not seeking to lift Himself up, He didn't even tell the man who He was! He knew it was His Father's future plan to glorify Him, but His earthly ministry was to serve man (Mark 10:45) by submitting to the Father (John 17:4). Even though Jesus was the Christ, He practiced humility. He preached with authority, love and grace, not arrogance and dictatorship.

Recently I received some books from one of my uncle pastors who was streamlining his library. As I was looking through them I was amazed to discover that many of his co-workers were famous pastors and theologians . Inside the covers were written personal notes to him from Billy Graham, Jack Hayford, John MacArthur, Walter Kaiser and others. I thought to myself, "I'm a pastor and seminary professor. How could he have worked with and befriended these well-known men of God without me knowing about it?" Then it hit me: he knew the value of humility and made it part of his Christian walk. He saw no need to brag about or even mention the important people he knew. God was the only one he would give glory to. He could know the President of the United States too, as far as I know.

Jesus was humble.

> "Blessed are the **poor in spirit**, for theirs is the kingdom of heaven. 4 Blessed are **those who mourn**, for they will be comforted. 5 Blessed are the **meek**, for they will inherit the earth. 6 Blessed are **those who hunger and thirst for righteousness**, for they will be filled. 7 Blessed are the **merciful**, for they will be shown mercy. 8 Blessed are the **pure in heart**, for they will see God. 9 Blessed are the **peacemakers**, for they will be called sons of God. 10 Blessed are **those who are persecuted because of righteousness**, for theirs is the kingdom of heaven. 11 "Blessed are you when people insult you, persecute you and falsely say all kinds of evil against you because of me. 12 Rejoice and be glad, because great is your reward in heaven, for in the same way they persecuted the prophets who were before you."
>
> - Jesus, Matthew 5:3-12

Thanks to David Betz 11-18-2005

JUST LOOK AT HIM ... HE TOTALLY THINKS HE'S GOD'S GIFT TO THE WORLD

He Challenged His Listeners

Last year my oldest son went to army boot camp. It was a wake-up call for him and for my wife and me as well! He was not allowed to receive any correspondence of any kind but mail, and he was only allowed to make one phone call in the first four weeks! Neither would his DS (Drill Sergeant) let the recruits have any CDs, DVDs, MP3s, TVs, VCRs or any other initials. He was not even allowed to have any books except the Bible, which he read daily, to my exceedingly great joy!

Life was hard for him. It was the first time he had been away from us for more than 2 weeks and he was struggling with the discipline and strain on his body and psyche. He even wrote us one time and said he missed his "mommy and daddy." What a tough letter to swallow, it left us heartbroken.

What made his training most difficult were the constant demands and challenges he received from his DS. Sometimes awoken in the middle of the night, never able to sit down to a meal for more than five minutes, and running with heavy gear on his back in the Georgia summer heat for miles all took its toll. Yet in the end, he appreciated these challenges--they helped make him a man.

My wife and I have often faced times when one of us needed to confront the other (albeit more gently). We found that it, too, was not easy, but normally in the end extremely beneficial, both to us individually and as a married couple. "As iron sharpens iron, so one man sharpens another" (Proverbs 27:17).

Shortly after the lame man had been healed and after he'd been questioned by the Jews, he was confronted by Jesus at the temple. Jesus warned him about the results of sin, "Stop sinning or something worse may happen to you" (vs. 14). Many within the holds of Christianity want to sing the praises of grace and freedom in Christ, yet fail to remember sin's consequences--in this instance, physical deterioration.

Jesus issued a challenge. The challenge was abrupt, fair and to the point. The devastating penalty of disobedience needed to be understood. The question now rising to the surface is, "How will people today hear the truth unless someone exhorts them?" The Apostle Paul echoed these words when he wrote, "And how can they hear without someone preaching to them" (Romans 10:14c)?

On a subsequent occasion when Jesus was foretelling His suffering and death to the disciples, Peter foolishly took Jesus aside and attempted to rebuke Him for His inconceivable forecast. Jesus returned the audacious favor by issuing another type of challenge in the form of a rebuke. He addressed Peter with alarmingly unforgettable words, "Get behind me, Satan! You are a stumbling block to me; you do not have in mind the things of God, but the things of men" (Matthew 16:23). Jesus held nothing back when it came to truth that needed saying. What a blow that must have been to Peter. Jesus had recently heard Peter's confession of Him as "Lord", and had addressed the disciple as the rock or a rock on which He would build His church (Matthew 16:18). Jesus had even said that he would hold the keys to the kingdom (Matthew 16:19)! But in spite of Christ's rebuke, Peter stuck with Jesus and truly became a "Petros" or rock in the Christian faith.

Jesus frequently applied confrontational challenges to those who wrongly interpreted the Scriptures and used them to their own advantage. One such time is found in Matthew 21, where the Sadducees, who didn't believe in the resurrection, asked Him questions about marriage after the resurrection. Jesus' reply to them was quite blunt, "You are in error because you do not know the Scriptures or the power of God" (v. 29). His point was clear--if they spent more time in the Word and less time evaluating each other's hypotheses they would find truth. Once again, His words were tough, but so was His mission.

Jesus challenged His listeners.

12-07-1999

TODAY'S CHILDREN'S SERMON IS ABOUT THE AWFUL AWFUL THINGS THAT HAPPEN TO YOUNG CHILDREN WHO DON'T PAY ATTENTION

He Prophesied

Jesus added to His elaborate arsenal of communication skills another weapon which most of us will likely never wield—predictive prophecy. He foretold of the resurrection to eternal life for the righteous, and resurrection to condemnation for the unrighteous (vv. 24-29).

He was able to *foretell* (prophesy about future events) and *forth-tell* (proclaim the things of God and the Scriptures). There are many great forth-tellers today who are revealing the written word, and rightly so, since it is commanded (2 Timothy 4:2) and cautioned (1 Corinthians 4:6-7). There is, however, great skepticism within the majority of the conservative evangelical Christian community concerning *foretellers* today, since they function very differently from those of Biblical times.

Those who do claim to be foretellers often carry out their work in a similar manner as psychics, palm readers, and astrologers--their predictions being so vague that they will likely make sense to anyone who wants to believe bad enough. Some even demand exorbitant amounts of money from folks, most of whom have very little to give.

The prophecies of these self-proclaimed seers should be viewed with suspicion, not only because of their ambiguity, but because of their personal excessive monetary and pleasurable demands, their desire for power, lack of connectedness with the church local and universal, and especially their inability or unwillingness to adhere to the boundaries of Scripture. Paul warned Timothy of similar men and also provided the remedy:

> While evil men and impostors will go from bad to worse, deceiving and being deceived. 14 But as for you, continue in what you have learned and have become convinced of, because you know those from whom you learned it, 15 and how from infancy *you have known the holy Scriptures*, which are able to make you wise for salvation through faith in Christ Jesus. 16 All Scripture is God-breathed and is useful for teaching, rebuking, correcting and training in righteousness, 17 so that the man of God may be thoroughly equipped for every good work." (2 Timothy 3:13-17)

Further, Paul told the Corinthians not to go "beyond what is written." (1 Corinthians 4:6) This Scripture reveals that the written Word (and of course the Living Word, Jesus) is all that is needed to mature in the faith and anything outside of it should be suspect. Such a thing as a "new word from the Lord" should certainly be subject to testing as the Apostle John implored: "Dear friends, do not believe every spirit, but test the spirits to see whether they are from God, because many false prophets have gone out into the world" (1 John 4:1). Please note that today's foretellers rarely wish to be accountable to or tested by a church body. Churches that have prophets need to test them more.

As for forth-telling there certainly needs to be more of that, particularly since *all* Christians are expected to witness. Jesus gave the Great Commission as the primary objective for His disciples, and it starts with preaching the Gospel.

Jesus prophesied.

REVERENDFUN.COM COPYRIGHT GCI, INC

Thanks to John LeBlanc 12-01-2006

IF YOU CAN'T PROPHESY ANYTHING NICE, DON'T PROPHESY ANYTHING AT ALL

Preaching the Seven C'S
Jesus' Sermon on the Mount

---

1. The Complements of Righteousness (His Beatitudes)

Matthew 5 (Luke 6:17-26)
1 Now when he saw the crowds, he went up on a mountainside and sat
down. His disciples came to him, 2 and he began to teach them, saying: 3
"Blessed are the poor in spirit, for theirs is the kingdom of heaven. 4
Blessed are those who mourn, for they will be comforted. 5 Blessed are
the meek, for they will inherit the earth. 6 Blessed are those who hunger
and thirst for righteousness, for they will be filled. 7 Blessed are the
merciful, for they will be shown mercy. 8 Blessed are the pure in heart,
for they will see God. 9 Blessed are the peacemakers, for they will be
called sons of God. 10 Blessed are those who are persecuted because of
righteousness, for theirs is the kingdom of heaven. 11 "Blessed are you
when people insult you, persecute you and falsely say all kinds of evil
against you because of me. 12 Rejoice and be glad, because great is your
reward in heaven, for in the same way they persecuted the prophets who
were before you.

2. The Conditions of Righteousness (His Standard)

Matthew 5
13 "You are the salt of the earth. But if the salt loses its saltiness, how can
it be made salty again? It is no longer good for anything, except to be
thrown out and trampled by men. 14 "You are the light of the world. A
city on a hill cannot be hidden. 15 Neither do people light a lamp and put
it under a bowl. Instead they put it on its stand, and it gives light to
everyone in the house. 16 In the same way, let your light shine before men,
that they may see your good deeds and praise your Father in heaven. 17
"Do not think that I have come to abolish the Law or the Prophets; I have
not come to abolish them but to fulfill them. 18 I tell you the truth, until
heaven and earth disappear, not the smallest letter, not the least stroke of a
pen, will by any means disappear from the Law until everything is
accomplished. 19 Anyone who breaks one of the least of these
commandments and teaches others to do the same will be called least in the

kingdom of heaven, but whoever practices and teaches these commands will be called great in the kingdom of heaven. 20 For I tell you that unless your righteousness surpasses that of the Pharisees and the teachers of the law, you will certainly not enter the kingdom of heaven.

3. The Complexity of Righteousness (His Ethics)

Matthew 5 (Luke 6:27-36)
21 "You have heard that it was said to the people long ago, `Do not murder, and anyone who murders will be subject to judgment.' 22 But I tell you that anyone who is angry with his brother will be subject to judgment. Again, anyone who says to his brother, `Raca,' is answerable to the Sanhedrin. But anyone who says, `You fool!' will be in danger of the fire of hell. 23 "Therefore, if you are offering your gift at the altar and there remember that your brother has something against you, 24 leave your gift there in front of the altar. First go and be reconciled to your brother; then come and offer your gift. 25 "Settle matters quickly with your adversary who is taking you to court. Do it while you are still with him on the way, or he may hand you over to the judge, and the judge may hand you over to the officer, and you may be thrown into prison. 26 I tell you the truth, you will not get out until you have paid the last penny. 27 "You have heard that it was said, `Do not commit adultery.' 28 But I tell you that anyone who looks at a woman lustfully has already committed adultery with her in his heart.

4. The Credibility of Righteousness (His Warning of Hypocrisy)

Matthew 6
6:1 "Be careful not to do your `acts of righteousness' before men, to be seen by them. If you do, you will have no reward from your Father in heaven. 2 "So when you give to the needy, do not announce it with trumpets, as the hypocrites do in the synagogues and on the streets, to be honored by men. I tell you the truth, they have received their reward in full. 3 But when you give to the needy, do not let your left hand know what your right hand is doing, 4 so that your giving may be in secret. Then your Father, who sees what is done in secret, will reward you. 5 "And when you pray, do not be like the hypocrites, for they love to pray standing in the

synagogues and on the street corners to be seen by men. I tell you the truth,
they have received their reward in full. 6 But when you pray, go into your
room, close the door and pray to your Father, who is unseen. Then your
Father, who sees what is done in secret, will reward you. 7 And when you
pray, do not keep on babbling like pagans, for they think they will be heard
because of their many words. 8 Do not be like them, for your Father
knows what you need before you ask him. 9 "This, then, is how you
should pray: "`Our Father in heaven, hallowed be your name, 10 your
kingdom come, your will be done on earth as it is in heaven. 11 Give us
today our daily bread. 12 Forgive us our debts, as we also have forgiven
our debtors. 13 And lead us not into temptation, but deliver us from the
evil one.' 14 For if you forgive men when they sin against you, your
heavenly Father will also forgive you. 15 But if you do not forgive men
their sins, your Father will not forgive your sins. 16 "When you fast, do
not look somber as the hypocrites do, for they disfigure their faces to show
men they are fasting. I tell you the truth, they have received their reward in
full. 17 But when you fast, put oil on your head and wash your face, 18 so
that it will not be obvious to men that you are fasting, but only to your
Father, who is unseen; and your Father, who sees what is done in secret,
will reward you.

5. The Commitment of Righteousness (His Ability to Care for Us)

Matthew 6

19 "Do not store up for yourselves treasures on earth, where moth and rust
destroy, and where thieves break in and steal. 20 But store up for
yourselves treasures in heaven, where moth and rust do not destroy, and
where thieves do not break in and steal. 21 For where your treasure is,
there your heart will be also. 22 "The eye is the lamp of the body. If your
eyes are good, your whole body will be full of light. 23 But if your eyes are
bad, your whole body will be full of darkness. If then the light within you is
darkness, how great is that darkness! 24 "No one can serve two masters.
Either he will hate the one and love the other, or he will be devoted to the
one and despise the other. You cannot serve both God and Money. 25
"Therefore I tell you, do not worry about your life, what you will eat or
drink; or about your body, what you will wear. Is not life more important
than food, and the body more important than clothes? 26 Look at the
birds of the air; they do not sow or reap or store away in barns, and yet your

heavenly Father feeds them. Are you not much more valuable than they?
27 Who of you by worrying can add a single hour to his life? 28 "And why
do you worry about clothes? See how the lilies of the field grow. They do
not labor or spin. 29 Yet I tell you that not even Solomon in all his
splendor was dressed like one of these. 30 If that is how God clothes the
grass of the field, which is here today and tomorrow is thrown into the fire,
will he not much more clothe you, O you of little faith? 31 So do not
worry, saying, `What shall we eat?' or `What shall we drink?' or `What shall
we wear?' 32 For the pagans run after all these things, and your heavenly
Father knows that you need them. 33 But seek first his kingdom and his
righteousness, and all these things will be given to you as well. 34
Therefore do not worry about tomorrow, for tomorrow will worry about
itself. Each day has enough trouble of its own.

6. The Criticism of Righteousness (His View of Judgment)

<u>Matthew 7 (Luke 6:37-42)</u>

1 "Do not judge, or you too will be judged. 2 For in the same way you
judge others, you will be judged, and with the measure you use, it will be
measured to you. 3 "Why do you look at the speck of sawdust in your
brother's eye and pay no attention to the plank in your own eye? 4 How
can you say to your brother, `Let me take the speck out of your eye,' when
all the time there is a plank in your own eye? 5 You hypocrite, first take the
plank out of your own eye, and then you will see clearly to remove the
speck from your brother's eye. 6 "Do not give dogs what is sacred; do not
throw your pearls to pigs. If you do, they may trample them under their
feet, and then turn and tear you to pieces.

7. The Character of Righteousness (His Conclusion - Prayer & Golden Rule)

<u>Matthew 7 (Luke 6:31-49)</u>

7 "Ask and it will be given to you; seek and you will find; knock and the
door will be opened to you. 8 For everyone who asks receives; he who
seeks finds; and to him who knocks, the door will be opened. 9 "Which of
you, if his son asks for bread, will give him a stone? 10 Or if he asks for a
fish, will give him a snake? 11 If you, then, though you are evil, know how
to give good gifts to your children, how much more will your Father in
heaven give good gifts to those who ask him! 12 So in everything, do to

others what you would have them do to you, for this sums up the Law and
the Prophets.
13 "Enter through the narrow gate. For wide is the gate and broad is the
road that leads to destruction, and many enter through it. 14 But small is
the gate and narrow the road that leads to life, and only a few find it. 15
"Watch out for false prophets. They come to you in sheep's clothing, but
inwardly they are ferocious wolves. 16 By their fruit you will recognize
them. Do people pick grapes from thornbushes, or figs from thistles? 17
Likewise every good tree bears good fruit, but a bad tree bears bad fruit. 18
A good tree cannot bear bad fruit, and a bad tree cannot bear good fruit. 19
Every tree that does not bear good fruit is cut down and thrown into the
fire. 20 Thus, by their fruit you will recognize them. 21 "Not everyone
who says to me, `Lord, Lord,' will enter the kingdom of heaven, but only he
who does the will of my Father who is in heaven. 22 Many will say to me
on that day, `Lord, Lord, did we not prophesy in your name, and in your
name drive out demons and perform many miracles?' 23 Then I will tell
them plainly, `I never knew you. Away from me, you evildoers!' 24
"Therefore everyone who hears these words of mine and puts them into
practice is like a wise man who built his house on the rock. 25 The rain
came down, the streams rose, and the winds blew and beat against that
house; yet it did not fall, because it had its foundation on the rock. 26 But
everyone who hears these words of mine and does not put them into
practice is like a foolish man who built his house on sand. 27 The rain
came down, the streams rose, and the winds blew and beat against that
house, and it fell with a great crash." 28 When Jesus had finished saying
these things, the crowds were amazed at his teaching, 29 because he taught
as one who had authority, and not as their teachers of the law. 8:1 When
he came down from the mountainside, large crowds followed him.

He was Calm

In this famous seven-part lesson, known as the Sermon on the Mount, seven more communication principles emerge. The first is rather unexpected. The passage informs us that when Jesus saw the crowds, He went up the mountainside, "sat down" (v. 1) and let the disciples come to Him. The very fact that Jesus would sit to teach all those gathered around Him implies a relaxed and calm attitude on His part. He did not allow the intensity of the moment to overcome Him and stress him out.

This was also true of Christ when He was in the fishing boat in the middle of the storm on the Galilee with the frantic disciples. He was so relaxed they had to wake Him up to tell Him about it (Matthew 8:23-27)! Oh that we could learn to let go of our plans and let God work His will through us!

A hospital can be a scary place for those who know they will soon be its residents. Surgery and treatments are often accompanied with pain and suffering and sometimes loneliness. Even the smell of the place is daunting.

I remember the apprehension I felt the first time I was told I needed to go "under the knife." My perspective had been that the hospital was a house of pain. The Lord was surely present with me, though, as I actually enjoyed my brief stay. Everyone working there did all they could to help me heal and feel comfortable. It didn't take me long to realize that what I had called a house of pain was in reality a house of healing.

The Lord gave me peace and contentment in what could have been a situation of suffering and anguish. The nurses even referred to me as a model patient—it was the Lord, not me, of course.

"You will keep in perfect peace him whose mind is steadfast, because he trusts in you" (Isaiah 26:3). Learn to trust God at all times—relax.

Jesus was calm.

Thanks to Ian (See Mark 4:35-41) 06-23-2006

JUST GIVE ME FIVE MORE MINUTES

He Amplified His Voice

It is likely that on the mountainside, Jesus amplified His voice. This is not a difficult task for most speakers, but it may be difficult for some to do consistently. In Matthew 5:1-2 Jesus sees the masses and is recorded to have gone up the mountainside where he preaches His longest recorded message.[53]

Communications experts tell us that sound waves fall,[54] so a speaker is better heard when speaking from an elevated position. This was a very practical reason for raising pulpits above congregations before modern public address systems. One exception to this rule comes from Roman architecture, the theater. In these half-moon shaped outdoor auditoriums it was not uncommon for speakers or actors to be heard from a lower position because of the funneling effect on the sound waves, and the lack of sound absorption by the hard surfaces (such as stone and concrete).[55]

On my first trip to the Holy Land, we were sitting in the theater at Caesarea Maritima. Our Israeli guide told us to be quiet and we would hear the people who were talking on the stage. To our amazement we heard their every word. At another larger theater at Scythopolis (at the foot of Beth Shan where King Saul's body had been hung on the wall) there were areas in the construction that resembled box seating. These were spaces where they placed barrels filled with water that acted as natural sound amplifiers.

According to Luke's account of this preaching event on the Galilean hillside (6:17), Jesus came "down" to a "level place" on the mountain to teach them. For some, this is a problem[56] since Matthew said Jesus went up the mountainside. The first possible solution is that Jesus spoke this sermon or lesson on more than one occasion and thus these are two separate situations.[57] However, Luke 6:12-16 clearly reveals that Jesus had earlier gone up the mountain to pray, He selected His twelve disciples, and then came down to the people. I think Matthew's account simply starts with Jesus going up the mountain and skipping to the sermon. Luke, however, has offered a detailed description of the whole event. Luke's description of a level place likely refers simply to the plot of ground where Jesus stood when He delivered His message.

From a communication perspective, there is still another consideration to keep in mind about Jesus' presentation. Luke's report states (in the NIV) that Jesus "looked at His disciples." Yet this is not a very good translation of the Greek word "*epairo*" as it means "to lift up, raise up."[58] So it is better understood that Jesus "lifted up" His eyes, possibly suggesting that He looked up the mountain at the people. If this is true, we would assume that He would have had to raise the volume of His voice and the crowd would have had to be incredibly quiet in order to hear Him. A fascinating Discovery Channel documentary revealed that on the mountainside where Jesus would likely have spoken, exists a natural theater, where a speaker can be heard quite easily from as far away as 400 feet![59]

The Apostle John records that when Jesus was teaching in the temple courts, He "cried out" to the people (John 7:28). The Greek word is "*krazo*" which simply means "to cry out" or "speak with a loud voice."[60] Jesus amplified His voice by raising it to guarantee that He would be heard.

Jesus amplified His voice.

He Offered Hope

I remember when I was 12 or 13 years old, I started working summers for my dad on his construction company. It was hard work "digging ditches." That is exactly what I did too. Back then, earth moving companies were not required to use sand around water and sewer pipes but could use about any soft fill available to encase them. My job was to shovel dirt by hand to keep rocks away from the pipe so they wouldn't break when they were backfilled and compacted. As you might have figured out by now, I was a grunt.

There was one thing that kept me going during those miles of ditch-digging in the dust and diesel—Friday afternoon and the hope of a paycheck. The expectation of getting rewarded for the hours of backbreaking labor somehow made it all worthwhile.

Back to Jesus' sermon, in verse 12 we find Him encouraging the faithful followers with His nine hope inspiring blessings or beatitudes, "blessed are the poor in spirit…" and concludes by offering a future to anticipate; "Rejoice and be glad because great is your reward in heaven."

Even though many of the folks we minister to today need to be challenged, provoked, even pushed--hope may be what motivates them best.

Jesus offered hope.

Jesus Made Eye Contact

Another skill Jesus employed in His teaching was eye contact. Luke 6:20 reads, "Looking at His disciples, He said…" Jesus obviously wasn't looking at the ground or up in the air, but at those to whom He communicated. When people wish to communicate something important, they look at each other, communicating with their eyes and expressions--maybe even with their hands. If the listeners don't look at the speaker it is questionable whether or not they are really listening and receiving the message at all.

Why do parents say to their children when they are demanding their attention, "Look at me when I am talking to you?" Is it not because they want their correction to be clear and memorable? They want to ensure obedience and respect.

When discussing the significance of eye contact, Bruce Wilkinson said, "…speaking is a contact sport."[61] In his workbook entitled, Teaching with Style, Dr. Wilkinson offers an "eyes chart"[62] to help his students discover effective and ineffective zones for the area the speaker is to look at when addressing his audience. He informs teachers that the optimum area is directly where the people's heads are in the center two thirds of the group.

In Mark 10:21 when the rich young ruler came to Jesus and asked Him about salvation, Mark tells us not just Jesus' verbal and emotional responses, but His physical response as well, "Jesus looked at him and loved him."

Jesus made eye contact.

He Encouraged Action

William Wilberforce was a man of words and action. At the age of twenty-one, he became a member of the English parliament and very influential in areas of reform. Because of his Christian faith and the influence of a former slave trade vessel captain, now an Anglican rector (John Newton, writer and composer of, "Amazing Grace"), he found the strength to invest twenty years towards ending the slave trade in his country. He was also responsible for the legislation that sent missionaries to India via the British East India Trade Company.[63] This one man's actions affected the morality and business of a whole country, and possibly a whole continent, even crossing over to parts of Asia.

"He wanted them to live their faith, not just learn it!"

On the mountain, Jesus issued a call to service. It was a specific and demanding call to the twelve as His elite group of personal disciples, and perhaps more of a general call to the many people gathered there hanging on His every word. He wanted them to live their faith, not just learn it.

He urged them in verse 16 to, "Let your light so shine before men, that they may see your good deeds and praise your Father in heaven." Jesus evidently expected His followers to be proactive in their faith. Likewise, effective Christian communicators should not just expose their research, they should encourage a response!

Jesus encouraged action.

IS THIS WHERE I GO TO GIVE MY HEART TO JESUS?

He Used Comparison and Contrast

A few sentences later, Jesus compared the righteousness of the religious leaders with that of His listeners (v. 20), "unless your righteousness surpasses that of the Pharisees and the teachers of the law, you will certainly not enter the kingdom of heaven." He wanted them to know a better righteousness than that of the Pharisees and went on to explain virtues like forgiveness and reconciliation (verses 22-23), commitment to marriage (vv. 27-28), and giving to those in need (Luke 6:30). He compared this new righteousness with a familiarly old and ineffective righteousness and exhorted that the new could "surpass" the old. The comparison of these two different concepts was a tool that enabled the people to follow His train of thought.

When Jesus taught the disciples about the dangers of money in Luke 16, He told them they would need to make a choice between whom they would serve--God or money, since, "either he will hate the one and love the other, or he will be devoted to the one and despise the other. You cannot serve both God and Money" (v. 13). Jesus demanded a choice from His followers in regard to these conflicting and demanding passions. This challenge caused them to think carefully about their own experience. Offering our listeners an opportunity to choose between options can be a very successful way to stimulate their intellectual involvement.

In Matthew 23:12, after teaching about humility, Jesus concisely summarized His thoughts: "For whoever exalts himself will be humbled, and whoever humbles him-self will be exalted." Before blasting the Pharisees for their pride and self-glory, He concluded with the contrast between the self-exultant individual and the humble one.

Jesus used comparison and contrast.

He Told Stories

Thirty-three of the top fifty books on the USA Today bestseller list at this time are fictional works or stories.[64] That is a remarkable sixty-six percent of all the genres available for purchase! Unmistakably, Americans love to read stories more than any other written form. People throughout history seem to agree, since nearly all cultures have their own great stories to tell. Most of them were handed down orally due to the rarity and expense of the written word (until Gutenberg's printing press, mid 15th Century). In fact, some scholars believe that even much of the Old Testament story may have been transferred generation to generation in oral form since there exists no evidence of Hebrew writing before the 10th Century B.C.[65]

Whatever the case, this was Jesus' most popular method for communicating His Kingdom news. According to Bruce Wilkinson's research, Jesus told stories sixty-five percent of the time[66] and possibly as much as seventy-five percent of the whole Bible is in story form.[67] Wilkinson further informs us that there are four areas where stories can be drawn or created from; experience, history, the Bible, and imagination.[68]

Jesus' stories were usually in the form of parables. Webster defines a parable as, "a brief narrative or story conveying a spiritual or moral lesson, or illustrating some spiritual condition or relation; an allegory."[69]

In the Old Testament there is just one word for parable and it is used sixteen times. Its meaning is close to Webster's definition, and may mean "proverb, poem, or a sentence of ethical wisdom."[70] In newer translations it may appear as a: "proverb" (Psalm 49:4; Proverbs 26:7, 9), "ridicule" (Micah 2:4; Habakkuk 2:6), "oracle" (Numbers 23:7, 18; 24:3, 15, 20, 21, 23) and "discourse" (Job 27:1; 29:1) depending on the context in which it is used.

In the Greek New Testament there are two words for parable. The first is found only once, in the account where Jesus compares Himself to a shepherd whose voice is known by His sheep (John 10:6). It means, "A proverb, a symbolic or figurative saying, an extended or elaborate metaphor"[71] and is translated "figure of speech" in both The New International Version and the New American Standard Version.

The word for parable which is used in every other instance in the New Testament is *para-bolay* where the English word finds its roots. *Para* is translated "beside"[72] as in "parallel lines" (two lines running alongside of each other) and *ballo* as "throw or place"[73] as you would throw a ball. It is further defined as "A metaphor, a comparison, an example, a proverb, or a juxtaposition (a placing of one thing by another)."[74] Jesus told parables as a means to make complex or misunderstood spiritual truths understandable.

One important characteristic of Jesus' parables is that they were always made up from real ingredients (people, places, plants, birds, etc.). He even mentions one person by name—Lazarus (Luke 16:19-31). Parables are always short stories, 250 words or less and they arouse the imagination. They're especially easy to remember.

Bill Prest explained that the word parable appears to be exclusive to Jesus and the Scriptures, and has not been used elsewhere in English grammar or literature unless as a reference to them![75]

The list of parables in the Gospels is long, but the stories themselves may only have as little as one sentence, Luke 6:40 for example says, "A student is not above his teacher, but everyone who is fully trained will be like his teacher." Sometimes Jesus used one, two or many parables to teach truth. Luke 6:39 implies that He told a single parable, "He also told them this parable…" where Matthew 13:3 clearly shows a collage of stories, "He told them many things in parables…" Later in this same chapter Matthew wrote that Christ's preaching on the Kingdom of God there by the lake was only in parables: "Jesus spoke all these things to the crowd in parables; he did not say anything to them without using a parable."

Since Jesus used parables so much, we would be wise to learn how to tell stories that relate the truth of Scripture as well. One practical suggestion is to learn Jesus' stories and others from the Scriptures. Another would be to pay careful attention to the methods and illustrations of good storytellers. Reading fiction, history, illustration books and various other genres can be quite helpful for expanding one's imagination and ability. Several resources and even organizations are available to help those who are looking to begin or expand their storytelling skills.[76]

The form of delivery of a story is also important. Telling stories from memory is most effective, especially with dramatic emphasis. Even reading aloud with such emphasis will make it much more acceptable and enjoyable to listeners. Try it, they'll like it.

Jesus told stories.

Thanks to Charles Dunleavy 08-01-2006

IS IT "PARABLES" OR "PEARABLES",
BECAUSE WE MIGHT HAVE A GOOD OPPORTUNITY
FOR SOME CROSS PROMOTION HERE

In the Know

Jesus Addresses the Cultural Climate

Matthew 11 (Luke 7:18-35)

7 As John's disciples were leaving, Jesus began to speak to the crowd about
John: "What did you go out into the desert to see? A reed swayed by the
wind? 8 If not, what did you go out to see? A man dressed in fine clothes?
No, those who wear fine clothes are in kings' palaces. 9 Then what did you
go out to see? A prophet? Yes, I tell you, and more than a prophet. 10
This is the one about whom it is written: "`I will send my messenger ahead
of you, who will prepare your way before you.' 11 I tell you the truth:
Among those born of women there has not risen anyone greater than John
the Baptist; yet he who is least in the kingdom of heaven is greater than he.
12 From the days of John the Baptist until now, the kingdom of heaven
has been forcefully advancing, and forceful men lay hold of it. 13 For all
the Prophets and the Law prophesied until John. 14 And if you are willing
to accept it, he is the Elijah who was to come. 15 He who has ears, let him
hear. 16 "To what can I compare this generation? They are like children
sitting in the marketplaces and calling out to others: 17 "`We played the
flute for you, and you did not dance; we sang a dirge, and you did not
mourn. 18 For John came neither eating nor drinking, and they say, `He
has a demon.' 19 The Son of Man came eating and drinking, and they say,
`Here is a glutton and a drunkard, a friend of tax collectors and "sinners." '
But wisdom is proved right by her actions." 20 Then Jesus began to
denounce the cities in which most of his miracles had been performed,
because they did not repent. 21 "Woe to you, Korazin! Woe to you,
Bethsaida! If the miracles that were performed in you had been performed
in Tyre and Sidon, they would have repented long ago in sackcloth and
ashes. 22 But I tell you, it will be more bearable for Tyre and Sidon on the
day of judgment than for you. 23 And you, Capernaum, will you be lifted
up to the skies? No, you will go down to the depths. If the miracles that
were performed in you had been performed in Sodom, it would have
remained to this day. 24 But I tell you that it will be more bearable for
Sodom on the day of judgment than for you." 25 At that time Jesus said,
"I praise you, Father, Lord of heaven and earth, because you have hidden
these things from the wise and learned, and revealed them to little children.
26 Yes, Father, for this was your good pleasure. 27 "All things have been
committed to me by my Father. No one knows the Son except the Father,

and no one knows the Father except the Son and those to whom the Son chooses to reveal him. 28 "Come to me, all you who are weary and burdened, and I will give you rest. 29 Take my yoke upon you and learn from me, for I am gentle and humble in heart, and you will find rest for your souls. 30 For my yoke is easy and my burden is light."

He Illustrated With Contemporary Information

The next method of communication that Jesus employed was the use of contemporary information. Matthew recorded Jesus quoting His critics for illustrative purposes, "For John came… and they say 'he has a demon.' The Son of man came… and they say, 'here is a glutton…'" (11:18).

Three verses later (v. 21) Jesus reminded the people of some of the local news, "the miracles that were performed in you." In Luke's Gospel (7:22) He implored more news as a defense to John's doubt, "Go back and report to John what you have seen and heard: The blind receive sight, the lame walk… and the good news is preached to the poor."

The Lord even made reference to the laws of the day. John 8:17 records His reply to the Pharisees who challenged His witness of Himself: "In your own law it is written that the testimony of two men is valid."

The Master communicator was contemporary in His approach. He used quotes, news and law to illustrate His teaching. Most people enjoy hearing and discussing recent events, particularly those that are of concern to them. Many even get fired up over topics like politics, sports and taxes! With a little reading, observing and collecting, this tool can become part of anyone's collection of communication resources.

Jesus illustrated with contemporary information.

12-10-1999

HERE YOU ARE, PASTOR BOND, YOUR INSTA VERSE QUOTE 2000 SATELLITE WATCH ... AND SHOULD THINGS GO WRONG OUT THERE, THIS BIBLE CONTAINS A CLEVER DEACON DISGUISE

He Worshiped Publicly

A little later, Jesus did something very common to a worship experience, He offered prayers and praise (vv. 25-26). But this was no ordinary worship service, and no ordinary place for prayer in a public gathering--for He was in the middle of His speech! He had just completed His woes and denouncements of the cities in which He had performed miracles (v. 20) and He continued on by offering what He called a "better yoke" (vv. 28-30). Perhaps this unlikely occasion was the best time to commune with His Father since the level of hate from His opponents was fierce and rising, and His message was so desperately needed.

One thing is for certain, prayer and praise is a possibility for any moment. Jesus exemplified it and Paul, by the Holy Spirit, agreed with it: "And pray in the Spirit *on all occasions* with *all kinds* of prayers and requests. With this in mind, be alert and always keep on praying for all the saints" (Ephesians 6:18).

I remember at the Urbana Missions Conference one year, Louis Palau spoke of his first experience with a prayer warrior who later became one of his mentors. In his humorous way with Spanish accent, Louis told how this man would passionately pray. He started with a list of local ministers and Christians, then prayed for unsaved people in the community. Just as Louis thought the man was about done, he got out another list and began praying for local missionaries. Then as Louis thought to himself, "Okay, we must be nearing the end," the prayer warrior pulled out a map of the world! Louis said he almost fell over at the sight of it, but as you might expect, his mentor kept praying for dozens of foreign missionaries. And if that wasn't enough, he pleaded with the Lord in great detail!

Jesus prayed in detail too. You can witness one of those prayers first hand in John chapter 17. He encouraged and applauded prayer, both public and private (Matthew 6:6). He was not ashamed to call on His Heavenly Father anytime, anywhere.

Jesus worshiped publicly.

A Prophet without Honor
Jesus is Disrespected in His Hometown

Matthew 13

54 Coming to his hometown, he began teaching the people in their synagogue, and they were amazed. "Where did this man get this wisdom and these miraculous powers?" they asked. 55 "Isn't this the carpenter's son? Isn't his mother's name Mary, and aren't his brothers James, Joseph, Simon and Judas? 56 Aren't all his sisters with us? Where then did this man get all these things?" 57 And they took offense at him. But Jesus said to them, "Only in his hometown and in his own house is a prophet without honor." 58 And he did not do many miracles there because of their lack of faith.

Mark 6

1 Jesus left there and went to his hometown, accompanied by his disciples.
2 When the Sabbath came, he began to teach in the synagogue, and many who heard him were amazed. "Where did this man get these things?" they asked. "What's this wisdom that has been given him, that he even does miracles! 3 Isn't this the carpenter? Isn't this Mary's son and the brother of James, Joseph, Judas and Simon? Aren't his sisters here with us?" And they took offense at him. 4 Jesus said to them, "Only in his hometown, among his relatives and in his own house is a prophet without honor." 5 He could not do any miracles there, except lay his hands on a few sick people and heal them. 6 And he was amazed at their lack of faith. Then Jesus went around teaching from village to village.

He Invested in the Faithful

There are only two times in the Scriptures where it is said that Jesus was "amazed",[77] once is here in Mark 6:6 and the other is in Luke 7:9 (where Jesus had met the Roman Centurion who told Him He didn't have to go to his home to heal His servant but to just say the word and he would be healed). This time Christ's astonishment was due to a lack of faith on the part of His own people, and in the other instance it was due to an overabundance of it on the part of a Roman soldier! For the Nazarenes, the result of this lack of faith was a lack of function. Jesus didn't do any miracles for them because they didn't trust in His authority!

"The result of this lack of faith was a lack of function."

Matthew informs us in 13:54 (and Mark 6:2) that the people were amazed at His "wisdom" and "miraculous powers." Even in their admiration and astonishment, they still "took offense at Him" (verse 57) and lacked enough faith to receive any miracles from the Messiah (although Mark says He did heal some of the sick, in verse 5). This prompted Jesus to utter the legendary words, "in his hometown and in his own house a prophet is without honor" (Matthew 13:57; Mark 6:4).[78]

The thrust of Jesus' ministry is certainly to those who sought Him and followed Him. He healed and performed miracles for those who trusted in Him and His Godhood. He also did these things for teaching purposes and authentication of His ministry and Messiahship. He worked closely with His twelve disciples for most of His ministry and according to Dr. Dann Spader in "Growing a Healthy Church," Jesus invested seventy-five percent of His time in their training and multiplication.[79] He further wrote that the profile of responsive people involves faithfulness, availability, teachability and enthusiasm.[80]

Faithfulness is the primary characteristic the apostle Paul encouraged Timothy to look for in his disciple-making. He wrote, "And the things you have heard me say in the presence of many witnesses, these entrust to faithful men who will be able to teach others also." (NASB) Jesus and Paul looked for faithfulness in those to whom they would invest their valuable time and energy. Should any less be expected by Christian leaders today?

Jesus invested in the faithful.

Handle with Care

Jesus Serves the People Out of Love

Matthew 9 (Mark 6)

35 Jesus went through all the towns and villages, teaching in their
synagogues, preaching the good news of the kingdom and healing every
disease and sickness. 36 When he saw the crowds, he had compassion on
them, because they were harassed and helpless, like sheep without a
shepherd. 37 Then he said to his disciples, "The harvest is plentiful but the
workers are few. 38 Ask the Lord of the harvest, therefore, to send out
workers into his harvest field."

He Cared About People

Eduardo was impressed. He witnessed love and compassion from our church members who traveled thousands of miles to help build his sister's new house. Her old, one-room shack was so low to the ground that when it rained the water had flowed into her one room home, often carrying with it the waste from the outhouse just ten feet away. The new house was built up on a mound several feet higher and made with cement blocks so it would remain high, dry, and sanitary.

Eduardo helped with the construction and enjoyed working with our crew. He soon realized that there was nothing in this difficult project for us Americans but sweat and tears--sweat from the extreme heat and humidity, and tears of thanks from his sister and her many children. Eduardo was so touched by the whole experience, that after we left, he soon gave his life to Christ!

Here in Matthew 9:36, Jesus' concern for the crowds is evident, "When He saw the crowds, He had compassion on them." The King James translated the passage as, "moved with compassion" and the New American Standard, "He felt compassion." All these translations are accurate with the original language since the original Greek word means, "to have compassion" or "to be moved with compassion."[81] The evident conclusion to this writ is that Jesus cared deeply about people.

John 13:1 reveals an even deeper level of Christ's love for His followers, "Having loved his own who were in the world, he now showed them the full extent of his love (Or he loved them to the last)." The New American Standard and the King James versions read, "He loved them (unto) to the end." The word for end in Greek is *tel-os'* which means, "end, termination, the limit at which a thing ceases to be (always of the end of some act or state, but not of the end of a period of time).[82] The indication is not that He was at the end of His love for them, but the end of His earthly ministry was near. His love would continue throughout eternity. Romans 8:39 affirms this truth; "Neither height nor depth, nor anything else in all creation, will be able to separate us from the love of God that is in Christ Jesus our Lord."

If true disciples of Christ are to be effective mentors, teachers and leaders, they must exercise compassion and love.

Jesus cared about people.

What You See is What You Get

Jesus Teaches About Greatness in the Kingdom

Matthew 18

1 At that time the disciples came to Jesus and asked, "Who is the greatest in the kingdom of heaven?" 2 He called a little child and had him stand among them. 3 And he said: "I tell you the truth, unless you change and become like little children, you will never enter the kingdom of heaven. 4 Therefore, whoever humbles himself like this child is the greatest in the kingdom of heaven. 5 "And whoever welcomes a little child like this in my name welcomes me.

Mark 9

33 They came to Capernaum. When he was in the house, he asked them, "What were you arguing about on the road?" 34 But they kept quiet because on the way they had argued about who was the greatest. 35 Sitting down, Jesus called the Twelve and said, "If anyone wants to be first, he must be the very last, and the servant of all." 36 He took a little child and had him stand among them. Taking him in his arms, he said to them, 37 "Whoever welcomes one of these little children in my name welcomes me; and whoever welcomes me does not welcome me but the one who sent me."

Luke 9

46 An argument started among the disciples as to which of them would be the greatest. 47 Jesus, knowing their thoughts, took a little child and had him stand beside him. 48 Then he said to them, "Whoever welcomes this little child in my name welcomes me; and whoever welcomes me welcomes the one who sent me. For he who is least among you all--he is the greatest."

He Used Object Lessons

I dare say that everyone at some point in their lives has had a strong desire to find approval from someone they cared for or revered. Also there is a desire among us humans to be seen as the best at what we do. The disciples were no different than the rest of us. They argued about this very subject and Jesus caught them doing it (Mark 9:33).

To calm the uprising about who would be the greatest in the Kingdom, Jesus used an object lesson. He called a little child to Him and had him stand among them. His answer to their selfish inquiry was, "whoever humbles himself like this child is the greatest in the kingdom of heaven" (Matthew 18:4). Jesus wanted them to understand humility so He put the innocent trusting child in front of them as a living visual aid. This undoubtedly burned an unforgettable image of humility in their minds. Object lessons are every bit as powerful for adults as they are for children. After all, even though the disciples were grown-ups, they were behaving very immaturely.

I often use illusions as Biblical object lessons when I speak to children or youth and it never ceases to amaze me how the adults respond. They appear to learn more from the lessons than the children do.

The laws that Moses relayed to the people of Israel from the LORD included a command to display them visually: "Tie them as symbols on your hands and bind them on your foreheads. 9 Write them on the doorframes of your houses and on your gates" (Deuteronomy 6:8-9).

Even modern education and communications researchers have concluded that visual learning has the highest retention level of all learning methods. Eighty-three percent of the information we retain relates to sight, eleven percent to hearing and only six percent to the other senses.[83]

Jesus even used nature for His object lessons. Mark records an odd and curious event that took place on one of their trips to Jerusalem. Jesus saw a fig tree without figs and cursed it. Then, "in the morning, as they went along, they saw the fig tree withered from the roots. 21 Peter remembered and said to Jesus, 'Rabbi, look! The fig tree you cursed has withered" (11:14, 20-21)! Jesus responded with a brief discourse on the power of faith, which unmistakably impressed His teaching into their minds' eye.

The Apostle John describes a time when the Scribes and the Pharisees attempted to trick Jesus by bringing a woman caught in the act of adultery (John 8:3-11). They asked Him what they should do since the law said she should be stoned. He reacted first by stooping down and writing with His finger in the sand. Then, as He continued to write, He told those without sin to begin the process of stoning. They all left eventually and Jesus told the woman that He didn't condemn her either, but warned her not to sin anymore.

Writing in the sand must have shocked the leaders of Israel. First, because they were so careful about who and what they touched for fear of uncleanness, and secondly be-cause it was not one of the standardized teaching methods for Israel's Rabbi's. John doesn't specify what Jesus wrote, just the result--His finger writing combined with His heart-searching challenge, remarkably shut them up and sent them home!

In His book, "Scribbling in the Sand: Christ and Creativity," Michael Card describes this event as a space in time;

> What Jesus did that morning created a space in time that allowed the angry mob to cool down, then to hear His word, then finally to think about it, be convicted by it and respond--or not. It made time stand still. It was original. It was unexpected. It was a response to the noise and confusion and business all around Him, yet it was not in the least tainted by the noise. Instead Jesus' action created a frame around the silence--the kind of silence in which God speaks to the heart. In short it was a supreme act of creativity.[84]

This supreme act of creativity undoubtedly resulted in a memory they would hold for eternity!

Jesus used object lessons.

A History Lesson

Jesus Teaches on the Sanctity of Marriage

<u>Matthew 19 (Mark 10:1-12)</u>

1 When Jesus had finished saying these things, he left Galilee and went into
the region of Judea to the other side of the Jordan. 2 Large crowds
followed him, and he healed them there. 3 Some Pharisees came to him to
test him. They asked, "Is it lawful for a man to divorce his wife for any and
every reason?" 4 "Haven't you read," he replied, "that at the beginning the
Creator `made them male and female,' 5 and said, `For this reason a man
will leave his father and mother and be united to his wife, and the two will
become one flesh'? 6 So they are no longer two, but one. Therefore what
God has joined together, let man not separate." 7 "Why then," they asked,
"did Moses command that a man give his wife a certificate of divorce and
send her away?" 8 Jesus replied, "Moses permitted you to divorce your
wives because your hearts were hard. But it was not this way from the
beginning. 9 I tell you that anyone who divorces his wife, except for
marital unfaithfulness, and marries another woman commits adultery." 10
The disciples said to him, "If this is the situation between a husband and
wife, it is better not to marry." 11 Jesus replied, "Not everyone can accept
this word, but only those to whom it has been given. 12 For some are
eunuchs because they were born that way; others were made that way by
men; and others have renounced marriage because of the kingdom of
heaven. The one who can accept this should accept it."

He Illustrated With Historical Facts

Another principle of communication that Jesus applied is found in verse 8 where Jesus used lessons from history to instruct his listeners. He answered the Pharisee's deceptive questions on divorce by stating, "It was not this way from the beginning." Jesus referred back to the roots of the institution of marriage in Genesis 2:24 as His proof text for its sanctity and stability--the creation of Eve for Adam and the resultant oneness.[85] Jesus made His case based on the facts of history, including the reason why Moses' permitted it: "their hearts were hard." (Matthew 19:8; Mark 10:5)

Later, in Matthew 23:37, after slamming the Pharisees, Jesus lamented over Jerusalem, "O Jerusalem, Jerusalem, you who kill the prophets and stone those sent to you, how often I have longed to gather your children together, as a hen gathers her chicks under her wings, but you were not willing." Jesus acknowledged a piece of Israel's sordid past--the stoning of her own prophets. Just a few verses earlier He condemned Israel's leaders for they were "sons of those who murdered the prophets" (v. 31). Jesus utilized this information to warn them and prepare them for the future.[86]

It has often been said that history repeats itself, and we can learn from the mistakes of the past to better our present situation and ensure a more hopeful future. History is a most excellent teacher for those who look to it.

Jesus illustrated with historical facts.

When Opportunity Knocks

Jesus Counsels a Rich Young Ruler

Matthew 19 (Mark 10:17-31; Luke 18:18-30)
16 Now a man came up to Jesus and asked, "Teacher, what good thing
must I do to get eternal life?" 17 "Why do you ask me about what is
good?" Jesus replied. "There is only One who is good. If you want to enter
life, obey the commandments." 18 "Which ones?" the man inquired. Jesus
replied, "`Do not murder, do not commit adultery, do not steal, do not give
false testimony, 19 honor your father and mother,' and `love your
neighbor as yourself.'" 20 "All these I have kept," the young man said.
"What do I still lack?" 21 Jesus answered, "If you want to be perfect, go,
sell your possessions and give to the poor, and you will have treasure in
heaven. Then come, follow me." 22 When the young man heard this, he
went away sad, because he had great wealth. 23 Then Jesus said to his
disciples, "I tell you the truth, it is hard for a rich man to enter the kingdom
of heaven. 24 Again I tell you, it is easier for a camel to go through the eye
of a needle than for a rich man to enter the kingdom of God." 25 When
the disciples heard this, they were greatly astonished and asked, "Who then
can be saved?" 26 Jesus looked at them and said, "With man this is
impossible, but with God all things are possible." 27 Peter answered him,
"We have left everything to follow you! What then will there be for us?" 28
Jesus said to them, "I tell you the truth, at the renewal of all things, when
the Son of Man sits on his glorious throne, you who have followed me will
also sit on twelve thrones, judging the twelve tribes of Israel. 29 And
everyone who has left houses or brothers or sisters or father or mother or
children or fields for my sake will receive a hundred times as much and will
inherit eternal life. 30 But many who are first will be last, and many who
are last will be first. 20:1 "For the kingdom of heaven is like a landowner
who went out early in the morning to hire men to work in his vineyard. 2
He agreed to pay them a denarius for the day and sent them into his
vineyard. 3 "About the third hour he went out and saw others standing in
the marketplace doing nothing. 4 He told them, `You also go and work in
my vineyard, and I will pay you whatever is right.' 5 So they went. "He
went out again about the sixth hour and the ninth hour and did the same
thing. 6 About the eleventh hour he went out and found still others
standing around. He asked them, `Why have you been standing here all day
long doing nothing?' 7 "`Because no one has hired us,' they answered.
"He said to them, `You also go and work in my vineyard.' 8 "When

evening came, the owner of the vineyard said to his foreman, `Call the workers and pay them their wages, beginning with the last ones hired and going on to the first.' 9 "The workers who were hired about the eleventh hour came and each received a denarius. 10 So when those came who were hired first, they expected to receive more. But each one of them also received a denarius. 11 When they received it, they began to grumble against the landowner. 12 `These men who were hired last worked only one hour,' they said, `and you have made them equal to us who have borne the burden of the work and the heat of the day.' 13 "But he answered one of them, `Friend, I am not being unfair to you. Didn't you agree to work for a denarius? 14 Take your pay and go. I want to give the man who was hired last the same as I gave you. 15 Don't I have the right to do what I want with my own money? Or are you envious because I am generous?' 16 "So the last will be first, and the first will be last."

He Used Teachable Moments

In this classic passage of the rich young ruler we find that the Lord took advantage of the situation to teach the disciples a worthwhile lesson about the entrapments of wealth. In educational circles, this is often called a "teachable moment." It is a moment in time where the learner is captive to a concept or matter they do not understand, and curiosity forces them to listen intently for the answer.

Jesus focused on the response of the young man who "went away sad," (v. 22) and introduced the disciples to the difficulties wealthy people have in following Him. He said, "I tell you the truth, it is hard for a rich man to enter the kingdom of heaven. 24 Again I tell you, it is easier for a camel to go through the eye of a needle than for a rich man to enter the kingdom of God." (vv. 23-24) The obvious immediate reply of the disciples was to ask who could be saved, and Jesus stated that it would take God's intervention, for with God, "all things are possible." (v. 26)

I remember the Boy Scout days. We had a lot of fun, but we also had to work hard to gain badges, sashes and bronze, silver and gold chains. Our troop was specially blessed with Mr. Nesbitt, a leader who enjoyed taking us wild small town boys out into the wilderness.

Living in Eastern Canada, there were many frigid nights, some very cold and some very wet. It was at times like these that we were particularly eager to listen to Scout Master Nesbitt's instruction about fire and shelter building. We all wanted to get warm and dry and we knew he was the one who could do it. We were teachable then, if not at any other time.

There is no question that teachable moments like this one are prime opportunities for learning. After all, it is the time when an inquirer is most curious about the subject at hand and most eager to listen and learn.

Luke 21:2 reveals another such moment for the disciples. "He (Jesus) also saw a poor widow put in two very small copper coins. 3 'I tell you the truth,' he said, 'this poor widow has put in more than all the others. 4 All these people gave their gifts out of their wealth; but she out of her poverty put in all she had to live on.'" What a powerful lesson on giving financially to God! Their observation of the widow's offering and Jesus' explanation of it was sure to make a lasting impression on them, just as it has on many of us some two thousand years later!

Jesus used teachable moments.

REVERENDFUN.COM COPYRIGHT GCI, INC

Thanks to Nick's Pastor 11-24-2006

THAT'S THE TROUBLE WITH LIVING SACRIFICES

A Promise Keeper
Jesus Reveals Himself as the True Vine

John 15-16
"I am the true vine, and my Father is the gardener. 2 He cuts off every
branch in me that bears no fruit, while every branch that does bear fruit he
prunes {The Greek for prunes also means cleans} so that it will be even
more fruitful. 3 You are already clean because of the word I have spoken
to you. 4 Remain in me, and I will remain in you. No branch can bear fruit
by itself; it must remain in the vine. Neither can you bear fruit unless you
remain in me. 5 "I am the vine; you are the branches. If a man remains in
me and I in him, he will bear much fruit; apart from me you can do nothing.
6 If anyone does not remain in me, he is like a branch that is thrown away
and withers; such branches are picked up, thrown into the fire and burned.
7 If you remain in me and my words remain in you, ask whatever you wish,
and it will be given you. 8 This is to my Father's glory, that you bear much
fruit, showing yourselves to be my disciples. 9 "As the Father has loved
me, so have I loved you. Now remain in my love. 10 If you obey my
commands, you will remain in my love, just as I have obeyed my Father's
commands and remain in his love. 11 I have told you this so that my joy
may be in you and that your joy may be complete. 12 My command is this:
Love each other as I have loved you. 13 Greater love has no one than this,
that he lay down his life for his friends. 14 You are my friends if you do
what I command. 15 I no longer call you servants, because a servant does
not know his master's business. Instead, I have called you friends, for
everything that I learned from my Father I have made known to you. 16
You did not choose me, but I chose you and appointed you to go and bear
fruit--fruit that will last. Then the Father will give you whatever you ask in
my name. 17 This is my command: Love each other. 18 "If the world
hates you, keep in mind that it hated me first. 19 If you belonged to the
world, it would love you as its own. As it is, you do not belong to the world,
but I have chosen you out of the world. That is why the world hates you.
20 Remember the words I spoke to you: `No servant is greater than his
master.' {John 13:16} If they persecuted me, they will persecute you also. If
they obeyed my teaching, they will obey yours also. 21 They will treat you
this way because of my name, for they do not know the One who sent me.
22 If I had not come and spoken to them, they would not be guilty of sin.
Now, however, they have no excuse for their sin. 23 He who hates me

hates my Father as well. 24 If I had not done among them what no one else did, they would not be guilty of sin. But now they have seen these miracles, and yet they have hated both me and my Father. 25 But this is to fulfill what is written in their Law: `They hated me without reason.' {Psalms 35:19; 69:4} 26 "When the Counselor comes, whom I will send to you from the Father, the Spirit of truth who goes out from the Father, he will testify about me. 27 And you also must testify, for you have been with me from the beginning."

He Offered Conditional Promises

In His landmark sermon about the Vine and branches, Jesus' unearthed the final principle of communication. Here the Lord offers His followers conditional promises having to do with remaining or abiding in Him. He uses the tiny conjunction "if" ten times in this chapter, and every time these promises are bound to the maintenance and perseverance of their relationship with Him. He has made it crystal clear to every believer that they must obey and abide in order to belong and be blessed.

The resulting promise is that **faithful believers can expect: answered prayer** (v. 7), **to bear fruit** (vv. 8, 16), **experience Jesus' love** (v. 9) **and the Father's love** (v. 10), **receive joy** (v. 11) **and friendship with Christ** (vv. 14-15), **love from other Christians** (v. 17), **a relationship with the Holy Spirit** (v. 26) and **a sense of belonging and security** (kept vv. 4-5 and chosen, v. 19).

I remember as a young boy how excited I would become when my mother placed a plastic gold star on a chart on the bathroom wall at night after I brushed my teeth. It was a reward for brushing all my teeth all by myself. My older brother and I would compete to see who could get the most stars on the chart. I suppose this was the first real "Star Wars" epic!

We were both so proud of those stars. Mom figured out that a few cents spent on some fancy stickers was well worth the motivation for us as kids to do something healthy. Her conditional promise of adding stars was the driving force behind our participation.

Conversely, I remember the supper table trials—green veggie consumption or early bedtime! I like greens now, but when I was a child I detested them profusely and my parents didn't accept that aversion (it's a good thing they didn't). Needless to say their pledge of an early evening retirement for me came true far too often!

The grading system employed by colleges and universities is a fine example of how conditional promises can work well to motivate pupils to learning and growth. If they will do all the reading and assignments, attend classes and write exams, even pay their bills on time, they will receive good to excellent grades for their efforts.

What about ministry contexts in less formal settings? What are some ways we might be able to offer rewards and warnings where rules and regulations tend not to exist, like pastoral ministry, youth ministry and teaching Sunday school? Maybe the best place to start is with Scriptural promises like those found in John 15.

Jesus offered conditional promises.

Jesus' 7 Laws of Communication

Throughout this book I have shared with you my discovery of over 50 principles and characteristics about Jesus' communication during His earthly ministry which helped to convey the Gospel and divine truth to His disciples and listeners. I would like to point out that all of these principles can be funneled into 7 main categories, I will call "laws." These ***7 laws*** are;

1. The Speaker's ***Consecration***
2. The Speaker's ***Character***
3. The Spirit's ***Counsel***
4. The Speaker's ***Content***
5. The Speaker's ***Creativity***
6. The Speaker's ***Connection***
7. The Speaker's ***Congregation***

The Speaker's Consecration

Four principles fit into the first law of The Speaker's Consecration. They are; *He knew the Scriptures, He Spent Time in Prayer, He was Faithful to His Calling and Gifts*, and *He Worshiped Publicly.*

These four principles relate to our need to be consecrated to God or to be set apart to Him and for His service. We need to maintain a close relationship with Him through a devotion to prayer, knowledge and application of the Scriptures, holiness, obedience and service. Jesus restated this truth when He advised, "Apart from Me you can do nothing." (John 15:5)

Just as a sanctuary is a place set aside for sacred use, so must we be a sanctuary, a people set apart for God's holy use. This should affect all our efforts at communicating the Gospel and the Word of God.

The Speaker's Character

The next very important law has to do with godly character and Christian living, and is consequently called, The Speaker's Character. There are five principles that fall under this rubric, they are: *He Expected Results, He Had a Good Reputation, He was Gracious, He Followed God's plan,* and *He was Humble.*

The Spirit's Counsel

In the grouping for the law of The Spirit's Counsel, there are four important principles discovered and discussed relating to the Holy Spirit's work through us: *He Shared Spiritual Truth, He Relied on the Holy Spirit, He Used Spiritual Sight,* and *He Exercised Spiritual Authority.*

The Speaker's Content

Under the section of The Speaker's Content, there are at least five ways the Bible can be utilized in ministry: *He Used the Scriptures, He Shared the Scriptures with Anyone, He*

Saves, He Read the Scriptures Publicly, and *He Prophesied.*

The Speaker's Creativity

Jesus was incredibly inventive and resourceful with His methodology and we should be too. Creativity will definitely help relieve the boredom people experience with preaching and teaching and may provide a breakthrough to their understanding. There are fourteen methods in this law of The Speaker's Creativity: *He Hooked Minds with Word Pictures, He Answered Questions, He Appealed to Truth, He Provoked Thinking, He Used Common Illustrations, He Asked Questions, He Testified About God, He Selected His Words Carefully, He Used Comparison and Contrast, He Told Stories, He Used Contemporary Information, He Used Object Lessons,* and *He Used Teachable Moments.*

The Speaker's Connection

Ten simple yet necessary principles fall into this skill section entitled, The Speaker's Connection: *He Repeated and Reviewed, He Got to the Point, He Summarized, He Made it Easy to Understand, He Made it Memorable, He Spoke with Authority, He Challenged His Listeners, He was Calm, He Amplified His Voice, He Made Eye Contact,* and *He Encouraged Action.*

In the final category of The Speaker's Congregation, there are eight principles relating to ministry to people: *He Meet needs, He Built Others Up, He Knew His Listeners, He was Passionate About Discipleship, He Offered Hope, He Invested in the Faithful, He Cared About People,* and *He Offered Conditional Promises.*

This masterful communication plan that Jesus Christ integrated into His ministry was powerful and life changing for His listeners! The great thing for us is that we can incorporate His approach as well, simply by exercising these laws in our preaching, teaching and counseling!

As Warren Wiersbe appropriately penned:

> He (Jesus) was able to attract and instruct all kinds of people in all kinds of situations, and He did it without the aid of the "gimmicks" that we think are so necessary for ministry today. There was a vitality to our Lord's messages that arrested the minds and hearts of His listeners... He turned His listener's ears into eyes so they could see the truth and respond to it.[87]

May Jesus' laws of communication revolutionize our lives and ministries. I hope and pray that His model of communication revealed throughout the pages of this book, becomes ours!

APPENDIX 1

Jesus' 7 Laws of Communication Outline

Law # 1 – The Speaker's Consecration:
He knew the Scriptures
He prayed
He was faithful to His calling and gifts
He worshiped Publicly

Law #2 - The Speaker's Character:
He expected results
He had a good reputation
He was gracious
He followed God's plan
He was humble

Law #3 - The Spirit's Counsel:
He share spiritual truth
He relied on the Holy Spirit
He used spiritual sight
He exercised spiritual authority

Law #4 - The Speaker's Content:
He used the Scriptures
He shared the Word with anyone
Jesus saves
He read the Scriptures publicly
He prophesied

Law #5 - The Speaker's Connection:
He repeated and reviewed
He got to the point and summarized
He made it easy to understand
He made it memorable
He spoke with authority
He challenged His listeners
He was calm
He amplified His voice
He made eye contact
He encouraged action

Law #6 - The Speaker's Creativity:

He hooked minds
He answered questions
He appealed to truth
He provoked thinking
He used common illustrations
He asked questions
He testified about God
He selected words carefully
He used comparison and contrast
He told stories
He used contemporary information
He used object lessons
He used teachable moments

Law #7 - The Speaker's Congregation:

He met needs
He built others up
He knew His listeners
He was passionate about discipleship
He offered hope
He invested in the faithful
He cared about people
He offered conditional promises

APPENDIX 2

Jesus the Rabbi

hrab-bee' - of Hebrew origin; 1) my great one, my honorable sir 2) Rabbi, a title used by the Jews to address their teachers (and also honor them when not addressing them).*

1. Jesus was called "Teacher" or "Rabbi" by other Rabbi's:

"Jesus answered him, 'Simon (a Pharisee), I have something to tell you.' 'Tell me, **teacher**,' he said". Luke 7:40

"Some of the Pharisees in the crowd said to Jesus, **'Teacher**, rebuke your disciples!'" Luke 19:39

"Some of the Sadducees, who say there is no resurrection, came to Jesus with a question. 28 **'Teacher**,' they said…" Luke 20:27-28

2. Jesus was called Rabbi by other people:

Andrew - John 1:38
Nathanial - John 1:49
Judas - Matthew 26:25, 49
Peter - Mark 9:5; 11:21
The blind man - Mark 10:51
The disciples - John 4:31; 9:2; 11:8
The crowd - John 6:25

3. Jesus lived like a Rabbi, they:

a. depended on others' hospitality; Lk 8:3
b. traveled as they taught; Lk 4:14-16
c. often had many disciples; Lk 19:37
d. were followed by disciples; Mt 17:24
e. urged followers to take the yoke of the Torah; Mt 11:29-30
f. were received into people's homes; Lk 10:38-42
g. a common treasury to which supporters contributed; Lk 8:3
h. used parables; Mt 13:3

* BDB/Thayer's # 4461 hrab-bee' - of Hebrew origin, A V -Master (Christ) 9, Rabbi (Christ) 5, rabbi 3; 17 1) my great one, my honorable sir 2) Rabbi, a title used by the Jews to address their teachers (and also honor them when not addressing them).

APPENDIX 3

Models of Communication

General Model:

Speaker	▶	Subject	▶	Student

Jesus' 7 Laws of Communication Model:

Speaker	▶	Subject	▶	Student
Character Consecration Counselor		Content Creativity Connection		Congregation

BIBLIOGRAPHY

Barna, George. *The Barna Report 1992-93.* Ventura: Regal Books, 1992.

Bilezikian, Gilbert. *Christianity 101.* Grand Rapids: Zondervan, 1993.

Card, Michael. *Scribbling in the Sand.* Downers Grove: InterVarsity Press, 2002.

Doan, Elanor. *Speaker's Sourcebook.* Grand Rapids: Zondervan, 1980.

Gardner, Paul D., Ed. *The Complete Who's Who in the Bible.* Grand Rapids: Zondervan Publishing House, 1995.

Hendricks, Howard G. *The 7 Laws of the Teacher.* Georgia: Walk Thru the Bible Ministries, 1988.

Havner, Vance. *The Best of Vance Havner.* Old Tappan: Flemming H. Revell, 1969.

Horne, Herman H. *The Teaching Techniques of Jesus.* Grand Rapids: Kregel, 1974.

Keener, Craig S. *The IVP Bible Background Commentary.* Downer's Grove: InterVarsity Press, 1993.

Lockyer, Herbert. *All the Teachings of Jesus.* Peabody: Hendrickson Publishers, 1991.

McKnight, Scot and Williams, Matthew C. *The Synoptic Gospels, an Annotated Bibliography.* Grand Rapids: Baker Books, 2000.
Nave's Topical Bible, Software Edition. The Kingdom Christian Scholar Library, 1995.

People's New Testament Commentary, Software Edition. The Kingdom Christian Scholar Library, 1995.

Robertson, A.T. *A Harmony of the Gospels.* New York: Harper & Brothers Publishers, 1922.

Robinson, Haddon W. *Biblical Preaching.* Grand Rapids: Baker Academic, 2001.

Samra, Cal & Rose. *Holy Humor.* New York: MasterMedia, 1996.

Spader, Dann. *Growing a Healthy Church.* Chicago: Moody Press, 1991.

Stacy, R. Wayne. *Where Jesus Walked.* Valley Forge: Judson Press, 2001.

Stewart, James S. *The Life and Teaching of Jesus Christ.* Nashville: Abingdon Press.

Strong, Augustus Hopkins. *Exhaustive Concordance of the Bible.* Iowa Falls: World Bible Publishers, 1989.

Swindoll, Charles. *The Grace Awakening.* Dallas: Word Publishing, 1996.

The NIV Study Bible. Grand Rapids: Zondervan Publishing House, 1985.

Thayer, Joseph Henry. *New Thayer's Greek-English Lexicon.* Wilmington: Associated Publishers and Authors, 1977.

Thomas, Robert L. and Gundry, Stanley N. *The NIV/NASB Harmony of the Gospels.* Peobody: Prince Press, 2003.

Vander Laan, Ray and Markham, Judith. *Echoes of His Presence.* Colorado Springs: Focus On The Family Publishing, 1996.

Vander Laan, Ray. *That The World May Know Video Series, Set 3, New Testament Faith Lessons: Lesson 15, The Rabbi, and Lesson 18, Living Water.* Colorado Springs: Focus On The Family Films, 1996.

Wiersbe, Warren W. *With the Word, a Devotional Commentary.* Nashville: Oliver Nelson, 1991.

Wiersbe, Warren. *Preaching and Teaching With Imagination.* Grand Rapids: Baker Books, 1984.

Wilkinson, Bruce H. *Teaching with Style.* Fort Mill: Walk Thru the Bible Ministries, 1994.

Wilkinson, Bruce H. *The 7 Laws of the Learner.* Fort Mill: Walk Thru the Bible Ministries, 1988.

Wilson, Clifford A. *Jesus the Master Teacher.* Philadelphia: Baker Book House, 1974.

Wyld, Henry Cecil and Partridge, Eric H., Eds. *Webster's Universal Dictionary, Unabridged Universal Edition.* Harver.

Endnotes

[1] Hendricks, p. 78.

[2] Forty-three percent of church attendees never read the Bible outside of church, and another 25% only read it once a week. Only 13% read it daily. Barna, p. 109.

[3] Or preaching style, the word homiletic comes from the Greek word *homileo* meaning "to give a public speech."

[4] James Stewart, p. 64.

[5] Gospel means, "Good news" and "The Gospels" are the first four New Testament Books of Matthew, Mark, Like and John which account for the "Good News" of Jesus Christ's death (for our sin) and resurrection.

[6] The NIV/NASB Harmony of the Gospels. Robert L. Thomas and Stanley N. Gundry. Prince Press, 2003.

[7] *Soon-ed'-ree-on* , the great council at Jerusalem, consisting of the seventy one members, viz. scribes, elders, prominent members of the high priestly families and the high priest, the president of the assembly. The most important causes were brought before this tribunal, inasmuch as the Roman rulers of Judaea had left to it the power of trying such cases, and also of pronouncing sentence of death, with the limitation that a capital sentence pronounced by the Sanhedrin was not valid unless it was confirmed by the Roman procurator. 2) a smaller tribunal or council which every Jewish town had for the decision of less important cases. Thayer, # 4892.

[8] See Appendix 2.

[9] Jesus did have disciples who were following Him at this point and He must have been teaching them in some detail about Himself and the Kingdom, but it is not written out for us to investigate (John 1:35-51)

Jesus also had previously cleared the temple and prophesied about His death and resurrection to the Jews who were present (John 2:13-22).

[10] A detailed word study of preaching in the New Testament, revealed that the term preaching is related to the Gospel ninety-nine percent of the time it is used, where teaching is always related to doctrine. Thus Jesus preached the Gospel to Nicodemus.

[11] Nicodemus helped Joseph of Arimathea with Jesus' body; "Later, Joseph of Arimathea asked Pilate for the body of Jesus. Now Joseph was a disciple of Jesus, but secretly because he feared the Jews. With Pilate's permission, he came and took the body away. 39 He was accompanied by Nicodemus, the man who earlier had visited Jesus at night. Nicodemus brought a mixture of myrrh and aloes, about seventy-five pounds." John 19:38-39

[12] Rhabbi = (*hrab-bee'*) of Hebrew origin, 1) my great one, my honorable sir 2) Rabbi, a title used by the Jews to address their teachers (and also honor them when not addressing them). Thayer, # 4461.

[13] In the NT it means one who teaches concerning the things of God, and the duties of man, la) one who is fitted to teach, or thinks himself so, 1b) the teachers of the Jewish religion, 1c) of those who by their great power as teachers draw crowds around them i.e. John the Baptist, Jesus, 1d) by preeminence used of Jesus by himself, as one who showed men the way of salvation, 1e) of the apostles, and of Paul, 1f) of those who in the religious assemblies of the Christians, undertook the work of teaching, with the special assistance of the Holy Spirit, 1g) of false teachers among Christians. Thayer, # 1320.

[14] Webster defines a teacher as "one who imparts knowledge, a trainer of the mind." P. 1530.

[15] Wilson, p. 23.

[16] *Say-mi'-on* means a sign, mark, token1a) that by which a person or a thing is distinguished from others and is known1b) a sign,

prodigy, portent, i.e. an unusual occurrence, transcending the common course of nature1b1) of signs portending remarkable events soon to

happen1b2) of miracles and wonders by which God authenticates the men sent by him, or by which men prove that the cause they are pleading is God's. Thayer, # 4592.

[17] Doan, p. 192.

[18] Earlier in John 2:18 we read; "Then the Jews demanded of him, 'What miraculous sign can you show us to prove your authority to do all this?'"John 6:14; "After the people saw the miraculous sign that Jesus did, they began to say, 'Surely this is the Prophet who is to come into the world.'"Jesus rebuked the Jews for seeking a sign in Matthew 12:39; "He answered, 'A wicked and adulterous generation asks for a miraculous sign! But none will be given it except the sign of the prophet Jonah."

[19] Webster defines a metaphor as, "a figure of speech in which a word or phrase is used to denote a description of something entirely different from the object, idea, action or quality which it primarily or usually expresses, thus suggesting a resemblance or analogy," p. 1006.

[20] An analogy is defined by Webster as, "a partial resemblance or agreement between two things." p. 59.

[21] An imaginative comparison using "like" or "as." A rhetorical figure and poetical ornament whereby one thing is compared to another. Webster, p. 1382.

[22] In education this is a time when a student has an interest in a subject and asks a question about it. This is an excellent time to teach the student due to his desire to hear the reply.

[23] Direct Marketing Workshop 2000, Marketing Department, South Carolina Baptist Convention.

[24] Thayer, #'s 2784, 2097, 1223, 2980 & 3656.

[25] Ibid., #'s 1321, 3100, 2605, 2727, 2085, 1317 & 4994.

43 Barna, p. 65.

[27] Ibid., p. 56.

[28] Nicodemus was also a member of the Sanhedrin, a Pharisee and a ruler and would have been accustomed to debate. Douglas, p. 834.

[29] Webster, p. 1247.

[30] Wilson, p. 129-130.

[31] 1 Timothy 4:13; "Until I come, devote yourself to the public reading of Scripture, to preaching and to teaching. "Ephesians 3:4-5; "In reading this, then, you will be able to understand my insight into the mystery of Christ, 5 which was not made known to men in other generations as it has now been revealed by the Spirit to God's holy apostles and prophets."1 Timothy 3:16-17; "All Scripture is God-breathed and is useful for teaching, rebuking, correcting and training in righteousness, 17 so that the man of God may be thoroughly equipped for every good work." Acts 13:15; "After the reading from the Law and the Prophets, the synagogue rulers sent word to them, saying, "Brothers, if you have a message of encouragement for the people, please speak." Revelation 1:3, "Blessed is the one who reads the words of this prophecy, and blessed are those who hear it and take to heart what is written in it, because the time is near."

[32] People's New Testament Commentary, p. 46.

[33] Keener, p. 272.

[34] Vander Laan, p. 6.

[35] Keener, p. 272.

---

[36] When teaching at Word of Life summer conferences in Scroon Lake, NY., 2005 and 2006.

[37] Robinson, p. 74.

[38] "Messiah" and "Christ" are used interchangeably in the New Testament and mean "anointed" or "anointed one". Messiah is a Hebrew word and Christ is the Greek transliteration. The term Messiah only shows up 2 times in the Greek New Testament, the NIV Bible and the ASV Bible (John 1:41; 4:25). In these two instances the King James transliterates the Greek word as "Messias." Messiah does appear two times however, in the KJV in the Old Testament (Daniel 9:25 & 26) where the other translations use "anointed" or "anointed one". The NRSV uses Messiah in all the places where Christ is used in the Greek New Testament text with Christ in parentheses. The term "Anointed One" is used 4 times in the NIV Bible and the same term is used uncapitalized 10 times.

[39] 1 Peter 4:10-11, "Each one should use whatever gift he has received to serve others, faithfully administering God's grace in its various forms. 11 **If anyone speaks, he should do it as one speaking the very words of God**. If anyone serves, he should do it with the strength God provides, so that in all things God may be praised through Jesus Christ. To him be the glory and the power for ever and ever. Amen."

[40] This is an example of a Synoptic Problem. This is when the Synoptic Gospels (Matthew, Mark and Luke) differ in their accounts of events. Three major types of criticism have emerged to deal specifically with this dilemma; Source Criticism (where the sources of information the writer's used is assessed), Form Criticism (an investigation of the Gospel tradition in the 20 year period before they were written), and Redaction Criticism (where the writers are seen as later theological editors who were not actually Matthew, Mark and Luke). Gundry & Thomas, p.p. 260-284.

[41] Havner, pp. 10-11.

[42] The Pilgrim's map shows the distance from Jacob's well to Galilee to be about 30 miles. This is the same distance He had to travel from Jerusalem where He spoke with Nicodemus to Jacob's well. These events could not have taken place immediately after each other since He traveled by foot.

[43] Nave, # 4795.

[44] "Christ was the Messiah, the Son of God, anointed." Thayers # 5547 Christos {khris-tos'} from 5548.

[45] Thayer, # 5548.

[46] Ibid.

[47] Thayer # 3008 leitourgeo {li-toorg-eh'-o} from 3011; 1) to serve the state at one's own cost 1a) to assume an office which must be administered at one's own expense 1b) to discharge a public office at one's own cost 1c) to render public service to the state 2) to do a service, perform a work 2a) of priests and Levites who were busied with the sacred rites in the tabernacle or the temple 2b) of Christians serving Christ, whether by prayer, or by instructing others concerning the way of salvation, or in some other way 2c) of those who aid others with their resources, and relieve their poverty

[48] Romans 12:6-8; 1 Corinthians 12:8-10; 12:28-30; Ephesians 4:11; and Exodus 31:1-5; 35:31-33.

[49] Samra, p. 9.

[50] Ibid., # 5485.

[51] Swindoll, p. 9.

[52] Ibid.

[53] Note that verse one says He began to "teach" them, not "preach" to them. The Greek word is *didasko*, which means, "to

discourse with others in order to instruct them.“ Further, there is no indication that this was anything other than a typical teaching time except for the lack of interaction on the part of the listeners. The text even says “the disciples came to Him” after He went up the mountainside, so was He addressing the multitudes or just the twelve, or maybe the seventy-two disciples or some multiple of them?

[54] Cain, Communications class notes, Moody Bible Institute.

[55] Ibid.

[56] Referred to as a "synoptic problem" where the synoptic Gospel accounts read slightly differently from each other and may be a problem for interpretation.

[57] Robertson, p. 48.

[58] Thayer, # 1869.

[59] Broadcast December, 2002 on the Discovery Channel entitled, “Jesus, the Complete Story.”

[60] Thayer, # 2896. Not to be confused with the modern English word “crazy” that it sounds like. “Crazy” has Scandinavian roots meaning “to break” and subsequently evolved to mean “mental derangement.” Webster p. 328.

[61] Wilkinson, p. 50.

[62] Ibid., p. A-3.

[63] http://en.wikipedia.org/wiki/William_Wilberforce

[64] http://asp.usatoday.com/life/books/booksdatabase/default.aspx March 8, 2007.

[65] *Ancient Alphabet Used by Ancient Israelites*, Bangor Daily News, November 10, 2005.

[66] Wilkinson, p. 82.

[67] John Walsh, Christian Story Telling Network. http://christianstorytelling.com/about.html

[68] Wilkinson, p. 82.

[69] Webster, p. 1006.

[70] Thayer, # 4912.

[71] Ibid., # 3942.

[72] Ibid., # 3844.

[73] Ibid., # 906.

[74] Ibid., #3850.

[75] Bill Prest has taught English and Literature in Christian schools for over 35 years.

[76] Some organizations that have great resources for story-telling are; Christian Storytelling Network – www.christianstorytelling.com/about.html, Christian Answers - www.christiananswers.net/evangelism/methods/chronological.html, New Tribes Mission - www.ntm.org, and Walk Thru the Bible - www.walkthru.org

[77] The Greek word for "amazed" is *thou-mad'-zo* and means, "to marvel, wonder, admire." Thayer, # 2296.

[78] He had said basically the same thing a year earlier in the synagogue there in Nazareth Luke 4:24, "no prophet is accepted in his hometown." John 4:44 also references this statement, "Now Jesus himself had pointed out that a prophet has no honor in his own country."

[79] Spader, p.35.

[80] Ibid., pp. 134-137.

[81] Thayer, # 4697.

[82] Ibid., # 5056.

[83] Freese, Christian Education class notes, Moody Bible Institute, p. 3.

[84] Card, p. 16.

[85] Being created in the image of God has great privileges, oneness is one of them. Just as God is three in one, man had the blessing of becoming two in one through marriage. See Bilezikian, p. 121.

[86] Matthew 24-25 is dedicated to prophetic events.

[87] Wiersbe, pp. 159-160.

CPSIA information can be obtained
at www.ICGtesting.com
Printed in the USA
FSHW020626110221
78468FS

9 781933 899893